What People Are Saying About This Book

I have known Pat since 1979. I have been married to him since May 24, 1980. For as long as I have known him, he has greatly valued the input from fathers in his/our life. He is one of the most loyal sons to his fathers I have ever met. He has always sought, with a passion, to be fathered as well as to father. Our life has been rich because of this passion we have both embraced. Our prayer is that this book will encourage many others to embrace this lifestyle with a passion.

Marcia Davis
Pat's wife

When I first met Pat and his family, it was evident that he and his family were serious followers of Jesus. They quickly became good friends, and we experienced growth in the Lord together for many years. This was a journey of personal healing for both of us, as well as a journey to equip us for greater service for our King. We both were severely challenged in our belief systems as it seems like the transformation of our minds, as Paul said in Romans 12:2, has been non-stop for us this entire time. It seems as if we have been constantly challenged in how we live and what we believe on a daily basis. This makes for great testimonies but is not easy to go through during the process, and Pat's humility has never been in question as he has responded to God's leading at every turn. As Pat states on the last page of this book, "we are on a journey" and God is the one who places sons and fathers in each other's lives, all in the context of family. It has been a great joy to walk with Pat and his family for the last 20 years, and if you look closely at what he shares with you in these chapters, you too will be able to bear good fruit in all your relationships.

Alan Alford
Senior Pastor
Grace Fellowship,
Cabot, Arkansas

I am excited about Pat Davis' new book Ultimate Sons. Having known Pat for over twenty years, I have seen firsthand how his life embodies his message in this book. I have mentored and ministered with him for years and have watched as God has changed his life. He has been a great friend. Pat and I have traveled together in many countries in both Europe and Central America ministering and have seen thousands of people touched by God. We all need spiritual fathers and sons.

Harvey Boyd
Pastor,
Grace Fellowship,
Cabot, Arkansas

I was just a baby in Christ when I met Pat and Marcia. Pat was serving as the Youth Pastor at a local church. I was a broken young lady from a broken home. I had no knowledge of spiritual things. What I knew is that I needed Jesus.

Pat and Marcia invested time in me; to love me, pray for me, and to be the example that I needed of living life as a Christ-follower. They taught me to seek the Lord in all things—trust Him in the sunshine and the storm.

We all need guidance, love, grace, acceptance, and someone to hold us accountable. These are things that parents do for us. Often, our earthly parents are not able to fill the need. That is when the Lord provides for us spiritual parents to come alongside us to sow into our lives; to help us grow in our walk with Him.

The Lord brought me together with Pat and Marcia to fill this role in my life. After 33 years, I continue to seek their counsel, and they continue to sow into my life. They have now sown life into my family. I am forever thankful to them for seeing the potential in me, and for loving me in my brokenness. I am forever thankful to the Lord for bringing us together.

Sandi Stade
A youth where Pat was Youth Pastor in the mid-80s

I have fathered many spiritual sons in my years of ministry, and one thing I can say about Pat is that he has a longing to be fathered, unmatched by most people I've ever met. Over the years, Pat has consistently submitted himself to the leaders of his ministries. Having a calling on his heart to teach, preach and lead, Pat has been faithful to follow, even through seasons of seeming invisibility. Through it all, Pat has stayed the course, allowing God to continue a work inside him toward maturity. Following each missed opportunity to fill a leadership position, Pat positioned himself to be fathered once again, and I believe his faithful obedience is bearing much fruit. The words you read in this book are much more than theories; they are the result of Pat's life. Pat has written about one of the key issues in the church and the world right now. There is an urgent call today for relationships that provide a healthy atmosphere of spiritual nurturing and authority, and Pat calls on each of us to actively grow into being fathered as well as becoming fathers ourselves. This is the true story of a spiritual son becoming a spiritual father who has trusted God with the timing of his life. Pat, I'm so proud of you.

Tim Baize
Pastor,
Grace Fellowship,
Cabot, Arkansas

Copyright © 2020 Patrick Davis
ISBN: 9798664133295
Library of Congress Control Number: 2020912574
Published in the United States of America

All rights reserved as permitted under the U. S. Copyright Act of 1976. No part of this publication may be reproduced, distributed, or transmitted in any form or by any means, or stored in a database or retrieval system, without the expressed written permission of the author and publisher.

Unless otherwise noted, scriptures are take from THE HOLY BIBLE, NEW INTERNATIONAL VERSION®, NIV® Copyright © 1973, 1978, 1984, 2011 by Biblica, Inc.® Used by permission. All rights reserved worldwide.

Scripture quotations marked NLT are taken from the Holy Bible, New Living Translation, copyright © 1996, 2004, 2015 by Tyndale House Foundation. Used by permission of Tyndale House Publishers, Inc., Carol Stream, Illinois 60188. All rights reserved.

Published by

www.BurkhartBooks.com
Bedford, Texas

Dedication

To all the people who have had a role in being spiritual parents in my life, including my natural parents. They had a tremendous impact on my life.

To spiritual parents everywhere, thank you, for what you do!

Last but not least, for all those desiring to be ultimate sons and daughters, I dedicate this book to you and each of your individual destinies.

Acknowledgments

I want to thank several people who have impacted his life, and without whose input, this book would be a small handful of pages. Or none.

First, no one has touched my life and taught me what love is more than my dear wife, Marcia. As this book goes public, we are about to celebrate our 40th anniversary together. She has loved the Lord for almost 50 years. Thanks, so much hon for all you mean to me and all of your inspiration over the years!

My children, who love God and have married spouses who do as well. I honor their lives and all the input they have given me over the years. I know they have and will continue to impact their world.

Barry Hall, for his awesome job of editing my book! I appreciate so much his heart and working with me to make sure that my heart was clearly presented in this process. I also appreciate his dear wife and family being patient with him during that time.

Steve Marston, for his labor of love in putting this book to audio. What a great job he did! It is refreshing and peaceful to listen to him read it. I could not have a Spanish issue of this book without my dear friend Pedro Ajanel. He translated it into Spanish and is at the time of this coming to a finish, also recording the audiobook in Spanish. Thanks to both of you, men, for what this means to me!

My many pastors who have touched my life and spoken into it. Pastor Alan Alford, my senior pastor, and friend for 22 years. You never accepted great with me and always looked for God's best. A heartfelt thanks for all you have meant to my family and me!

Pastor Tim Baize, you have been so amazing as a father/mentor/friend for almost 20 years. Thanks for all I have learned about loving Jesus and how to love and father others! Thanks for how you've touched my whole family too!

Pastor Harvey Boyd, what can I say? We've traveled a piece of the world together and watched God heal thousands! Thanks for all of your patience, guidance, friendship, and trust with me! We will touch more of the world together in the years to come!

Pastor Melissa Younge, you have touched my life with your practical, loving ways, and I always look forward to your teaching. You have impacted my kids dramatically as well and have been a great example of a spiritual parent for them.

Thanks to all the elders, pastors, teachers, and leaders who have impacted my life over the years. There are way too many to name!

All my Bible college teachers, especially Rev. Don Meyer, who was such a blessing to me and married Marcia and I. Many of my other heroes from North Central Bible College (now NCU) have gone to be with the Lord.

The many youth over the years who impacted my life and groomed me for deeper ministry as their youth pastor.

My friends and family around the world whom I love and owe a debt of gratitude to for all I have received over the years. This includes my Grace Fellowship family, and you all know who you are.

Finally, of course, my best friend and savior Jesus, who is good all the time and has called us all into a crazy and wild adventure called the kingdom!

Contents

What People Are Saying About This Book and Its Author
Dedication
Acknowledgments

1 How This All Began	13
2 I Wouldn't Be Me	19
3 Blind Spots and Two-Way Streets	27
4 Father Knows Best	33
5 They Have My Back	41
6 The Defense Rests	57
7 The Difference Between "Why?" and "How High?"	65
8 Spiritual Armor Bearers	75
9 Honoring and Serving	83
10 Learner vs. Teacher	91
11 The Leader's Picture	99
12 Where Do We Go from Here?	107

About the Author

1

HOW THIS ALL BEGAN

Recently, I was reading a book written by one of my Bible college professors. As I read, a thought occurred to me that would ultimately become the basis for this book. I asked myself, "Why do I have so many awesome spiritual fathers and mothers who speak into my life who have impacted it so greatly?" I felt that the Lord spoke to me immediately this response: "It is because you desire to be a great son!" I considered this for some time. I do want to be the best son I am able to be. I want to receive everything that I possibly can from as many leaders whom God has strategically placed in my life. I could not thank all of them on this page. I would likely need chapters!

For instance, my college experience allowed me to interact with some truly unique and amazing professors. I would sit and listen to their stories for hours, reflecting on the ways that God used them to shape their world. One of my favorites was a man by the name of David Owen. He was a man that God used mightily in the Welsh Revival. He was full of stories about riding his bike all over Wales while preaching the good news of the gospel. His strong brogue always fascinated me. But what attracted me most was his heart for God, which drew me like a magnet to his side with my ears wide open.

Do you know what I learned from him? That I didn't know it all! From that point on, I made a decision always to have "big ears" to hear men and women of God who knew something that I didn't. (This simple point of motivation is a massive key to becoming an ultimate son or daughter, and I will address it more in later chapters.) We have to choose to become a student, or we will merely rehash what we already know. That would make for some pretty boring conversations after a while!

TOXIC FAITH VS. TOXIC CHURCH

I have often reflected on my experience with different leaders and spiritual fathers. I have noticed, over the course of many years, that developing and keeping strong relationships with leaders is not common to modern Christianity. Why is this?

"Toxic faith" was a concept that became pretty popular in the 1990's. Stephen Arterburn's book, *Toxic Faith: Experiencing Healing from Painful Spiritual Abuse*, was probably the most well-known piece of literature on the topic.

Arterburn addressed a trend of heavy-handed leadership styles that were present in some church cultures. His main concern was that people were being influenced by religion rather than by loving God – certainly an appropriate distinction to make. While the specific abuses laid out in this book were valid, I believe that an unintended consequence followed. Rather than reinstating a healthy culture of spiritual sonship as modeled in scripture, many began to cry "toxic faith!" whenever a leader spoke strongly into their life about anything. I contend that *most* of what was thereafter labeled as "toxic faith" was (still is) a deeper issue in the body of Christ that stands in contrast to the way that Father God intends for us to grow through relationship. God has not intended leaders to "lord influence over their people." On the other hand, God calls us into places of trust in others where the importance of receiving feedback and correction is a part of our character development in Christ. An inability to vulnerably trust will perpetually bear the bad fruit of shallow or broken relationships.

As a former youth pastor, I have had plenty of experiences with different leadership styles. For instance: I led one youth group that experienced significant growth, but I noticed an interesting pattern in my former pastor. Rather than celebrating what God was doing in the young people that attended his congregation, he became threatened by *me personally*. My success caused him to view me as his competition, rather than a co-laborer. It is difficult to partner with someone who has their defenses up toward you! In retrospect, I can share with you that this was a "toxic" situation. I did not desire their leadership position. Insecurity has destroyed many relationships.

Let me state clearly that there will likely always be leaders who do not represent the nature of God. Many such leaders misrepresent God by lording influence over their people rather than serving with grace and humility. But the response to this reality should never be to "throw the baby out with the bathwater." In some church cultures, this has become the standard.

I believe that "toxic faith" did two things: first, it exposed some real faults that existed in some specific movements and circles within the body of Christ. But second, it called spiritual leadership (fathering and mothering) into question at large, leaving a suspicious and defensive church culture in the place of genuine healthy leadership cultures. I see more and more believers rejecting the influence of those who have gone before them.

Insecure, defensive relationship styles can present from the bottom-up or from the top-down. In both cases, I call this malady *toxic church syndrome*.

For example: as good, godly leaders see the call of God on our lives, they begin to give us input about it. God uses some pretty uncomfortable circumstances to mold us and make us into who we are called to be sometimes. Unfortunately, and especially when we are offered input during difficult times, spiritual fathers and mothers can be misunderstood as controlling or overbearing.

When believers are unwilling to accept that spiritual fathers and mothers often see something that God sees, character issues are left without formation. At worst, this can even keep someone from stepping into their destiny in God, or stepping into their destiny only to have character issues mar their life's work.

WEIGHT ROOMS AND WAITING ROOMS

Resistance can be an important tool in building strength. Anyone who has engaged in some type of physical training, like going to the gym or running, can testify to this. But resisting spiritual insight during times of uncertainty does not tend to result in greater strength. Quite the opposite! When we are in the "waiting room," spiritual parents often offer insight into what Father God may have next for us. He always intends to take us to new places in our trust-journey with Him.

As a leader, I repeatedly have sons and daughters in my ministry who believe that hearing God happens in a vacuum - without any input. It is a hard experience when someone I love refuses to allow me to speak into their lives. I have heard remarks including, "I have the Holy Spirit, He will teach me, I do not need a teacher in this situation," etc. They love God; I don't question that. But they don't want to welcome spiritual fathers and mothers into their lives, or at least not when their input is hard to hear.

Pain often breeds an unhealthy need to control when what we could use most during trying times is the input of trusted advisors. I have seen people's resistance to a leader's input stunt their growth and extend the amount of time they spend in the wilderness. These situations break the hearts of spiritual fathers and mothers who only want to see God's best for the lives of those who would follow them.

Sons and daughters who refuse the input of caring leaders are often those who go from church to church, ministry to ministry, most often at the expense of their marriage, family, or both. Where is the next revival, the next night of worship, the next healing crusade, the next?

Ministry is exciting! Discipleship and growth? Not always so much. I have no problem with going to meetings where God's presence is real and impacting. Some people just do so at the expense of other important things in their life. If this has been a picture of your life, please be open to the pages of this book.

I have had to grow into this place of love and honor for the authority over me. It wasn't always that way (I'll say more about that later.) It is also my hope that those of you who welcome and honor the leaders that God has placed over you will be encouraged to continue in this, and even more so. As we have come to know by experience, God has so much good to share with us through these fathers and mothers.

DISCIPLESHIP AND FATHERING

Before we go any further, I would like to make a distinction between discipleship and fathering. Discipleship, in its strictest meaning, describes a learner under discipline.

People can disciple others even if they have not been a Christian for long. For instance, Paul told Timothy that he should entrust what he was taught to others so that they could, in turn, pass these things on to even more people (2 Timothy 2:2). But a father or mother is someone who, along with discipleship, also brings a gift of wisdom from experience into the picture. How does Paul distinguish between the two?

Compare the previous scripture to the following insight, which he shared with the Corinthians: he told them that they had ten thousand teachers (discipleship), but not many fathers. What was he saying? He was expressing his deep affection for them as one who carries them in his heart like a parent (1 Corinthians 4:15).

As you read this offering, I hope that you find yourself challenged and encouraged to press-in to those people in your life who carry you in their hearts—those fathers and mothers. After all, "When a student is ready, a teacher can arrive."

2

I WOULDN'T BE ME

I have heard the word *paradox* defined as "two seemingly opposing ideas contained in the same truth." Die to self to live in Christ ... the greatest must become the least ... etc.

At the outset of this book on becoming "ultimate sons and daughters," I want to draw your attention to one important paradox. For the sake of brevity, let's refer to this vast mystery as simply "Christ in me."

As believers in Jesus Christ, we have become a dwelling place of God.

WOW. Within this bottomless reality, a question must arise: who is supposed to be in charge here? If my life were a car, did Jesus enter as a passenger or a driver? This is a mystery that has caused quite a bit of confusion in the body, especially when taken to extremes. As one of my pastors says, "there are ditches on both sides."

One of these ditches sounds like this, "Everything that happens is completely God's will because God is in total control of everything in my life." Isn't that the song we sing: "... *More of you and less of me, Jesus* ...." It sounds very nice and is pretty easy to regurgitate in Sunday school. But there is a problem. This approach to the Lordship of Jesus will ultimately lead to the belief that "I don't matter." After all, if God is *everything*, and I am *nothing*, what should I ever expect to offer in partnership with Him?

The opposite ditch is evident, then: "It's all me." Yet I propose that we have been given a broad, smooth road between these two ditches. This road gives us a healthy understanding of our relationship with God and provides a balance of our relating to, and partnering with Him.

My wife and I have led a homegroup in our local church for 18 years. We saw and heard a lot of interesting things in those years!

One core thread we have implemented consistently is a commitment to encourage others to lead and participate in the growth of the homegroup. One night, I asked a man to lead a book discussion. When we were finished, we took the opportunity to offer him feedback. I thanked him and told him that he had done a great job. After I shared this, he said, "It wasn't me. It was the Lord." I chuckled and said to him, "I don't know, I was pretty sure I heard your voice a few times tonight."

If you have been a believer for any length of time, you have probably heard a similar refrain from fellow Christians. "It wasn't *me*; it was *all Him*." This has been a stronghold of thought for many believers who don't realize how uniquely valuable they are to His purposes. Whether from false humility or a genuine misunderstanding of God's ways, a more accurate description would go like this: "It's all me, and it's all Him! We're both all in!"

In the context that God is inviting us to partner with Him, we should consider the impact our decisions have on others. My decisions don't just affect me, but those around me as well. What would the New Testament look like if Paul had said, "Aw shucks, I'm just a sinner saved by grace, what could I ever have to offer here? God bless. Bye-bye now." Do you realize just how powerfully God can use you to expand His Kingdom, and become a blessing in the lives of those He has placed in your life? What a privilege!

Father God strategically places people in our lives—to offer guidance, prayer, companionship, correction—and these people are of such immense value to Him. And so much of my journey to become everything God intends is wrapped up in my connection to wonderful spiritual fathers and mothers. Don't get me wrong: without them, I could still be a man of God, a blessing to people, etc. I am talking about potential here. Fathers help us to see who we are, what our purpose is, and provide us relationship and feedback that are vital to our growth as sons and daughters.

As I address fathers and mothers in this book, I will often merely say "fathers." It is to be understood that both spiritual fatherhood and sonship are non-gender topics.

As it has been said, women can be sons temporarily if men are to be the bride eternally.

Learning from The Three Stooges

Curly has always been my favorite of *The Three Stooges*. In one of my favorite episodes, Curly is wearing a silly gorilla costume, while Moe and Larry confuse him for an actual gorilla who is standing nearby. Trying to clue his friends in, he shouts, "I'm not me!" I've always gotten a laugh from that. But more than just comedy, the Lord seems to highlight this moment to me over and again through the years. This scene mirrors how Christians can become confused about their identities, even leading others to confusion.

I submit to you the possibility that "I'm not me," or perhaps "I haven't become the full *me* yet," will be the echo of too many when they reflect on the way that they lived. I am speaking of lives that did not reach their full potential in Christ. This is a strong statement, so let me tell you why I might say such a thing. Yes, it has everything to do with family! As I welcome fathers and mothers into my life, "I'm not *me*" becomes "I am the '*me*' that I was created to be."

It is so much fun to watch people become who they are meant to be in the Lord. There is such freedom when sons begin to walk in their true identity. As sons discover their destiny, their outlook on life changes. Their desire to see their goals and dreams pursued becomes alive again. Those who have given up all hope begin to dream again. Fathers and mothers help us see the destiny for our lives, and help us run after it with their wisdom, prayer, and companionship.

God always allows me to choose His role in my life, in small and large instances. One thing is clear: as I allow Him to lead, my life takes the shape of what He intends. He leads us personally and intimately into purpose and destiny. One of the biggest keys to this reality is my choice to embrace the people He brings into my life – both to father me and also for me to father.

Looking Past the Good and the Bad

I have no idea where I would be without the fathers God has placed in my path. My connection with God today would have so many gaps if they were absent from my life. I have not always been able to see and appreciate their input.

There was a time in my life when I was driven by performance and gifting, and yet character issues were poised to destroy me. For instance, I will never forget the day when my pastor, Alan Alford, offered me a ride home from his house. I'm thinking that I may have been helping him do some roofing or something at his own house. As he drove me home, he spoke to me about becoming a home group leader. I was excited and eager to take on this role of leadership. However, Alan sensed something he didn't like in my ambition (which I admit, was not entirely healthy at the time), and could see that something wasn't right. He courageously changed plans, placing my wife Marcia over the group and not me. It was made very clear that she alone was to lead the group—ouch!

Let me say this: my wife is amazing, and anyone would be wise to join anything she is leading. But this stung a bit! Over time, as my pastors and community walked with me in dealing with some of these deeper issues, our leadership model was able to shift so that we could lead together.

I will never forget how this powerful experience taught me what it looks like when a godly father cares more about a person than their ministry.

My natural "male-brained" instinct was to think that my leadership was against me, and I built a case against them in my mind. I lived in offense for a time after that. In retrospect, I see now that Pastor Alan's priority was entirely protective. He could have let me go on to lead the group, but it would have likely resulted in damage to me, my family, and the small group. I am so grateful to Alan for looking past my gifting and my desire. Instead, he cared for me as a person. A father is not punishing. A father is not in a hurry. A father is able to take a longer view of the matter at hand for the good of all.

Now, many years later, I have also had the privilege to father others in the faith. As I consider those whom God has brought into my life, I see their gifts and passion for the Lord. I also see, at times, character flaws that will ultimately bring them pain if not addressed. Fathers have a great ability to see past the gifting into the very person who has been given those gifts. In essence, a shepherd helps his or her sheep to grow and steward the gifting God has placed in them.

God has such an amazing plan for our lives, and I believe this reality more today than I ever have! As I think about how my understanding of His ways has changed, I am brought to tears. God is a good, good father. He can be nothing less. He knows no shortage of love or grace. I can turn to Him and receive what I need at any moment.

Faithful Wounds

Sometimes a spiritual father brings direction and protection into our life, as I have just illustrated. Sometimes what we need is a spiritual father who will speak into our lives and bring a word of correction. Years ago, while I was working on a project with some friends, I lost my temper with Marcia. I was verbally tearing her down—my wife!—in front of one of them. (It was the first time, and last time, I ever made a negative comment about my wife in public. I wasn't proud of it.) One of my fathers in the Lord took the opportunity to speak to me about this. I listened to him, carefully considering his counsel. I was so deeply convicted!

His input saved us so much pain in our marriage, and also established a guideline that I would never cross again as a husband.

Now, so many years later, I am amazed any time I hear a husband talk negatively about his wife. I shudder to think about the many harmful words I might have spoken over the years if not for this timely rebuke from this father, this friend.

One of my favorite Bible verses is Proverbs 27:6, which says, *"Faithful are the wounds of a friend."* I assure you that it was not fun receiving this correction at the moment, but it changed my life! How often I have been "wounded" by loving fathers as they see something I don't see!

Encouraged in the Darkest Hours

On the other hand, a father has a unique ability to speak a word of encouragement to help us through difficult times. This entire book could not contain the encouraging words that have been spoken over our family by prophets, pastors, fathers, friends, family members, and others. At times when our emotions would have led us to ruin, especially in our early years, they were there to encourage us on.

There was a time when our daughter was going through a horrible ordeal with Lyme disease. She was very sick, and we could not see the light at the end of the tunnel. At the same time, our son went through a terrible divorce. Marcia and I were exhausted and broken-hearted.

These experiences were further complicated by what we were seeing in the lives of others, as we continued to pour ourselves out in ministry. We are privileged to be a part of a dynamic healing ministry through our local church, where we have witnessed amazing displays of God's awesome power and love. We have seen and often participated in the healing of hundreds of cancers, not to mention Alzheimer's, Parkinson's, AIDS, diabetes, blindness, deafness, and a host of other illnesses. That said, watching our daughter suffer for years with this illness was so saddening and conflicting. And watching our son go through an ugly divorce, while we see so many marriages put back together by the power of Holy Spirit, was terribly hard to bear. How could we reconcile that chasm between the answered prayers and the un-answered ones?

During this season, our spiritual fathers saw our circumstances and how we were affected. They were intentional to meet with us, encourage us, and ensure that we were not left alone in sorrow. They came near to us in this difficult time, and their presence meant so much.

As parents, we taught our kids to love the Lord. As long as I can remember, worship always filled our house. We constantly encouraged them that God had a good plan for their lives–they were champions. Royalty. Witnessing their struggles was more than a parenting difficulty; it challenged our theology. Questions like: Where did we miss something with our kids, or What did we do wrong, really haunted us in moments like this. If not for the loving words from our fathers, I don't know where we would be. Their commitment to us and to God's goodness over us helped us reframe this story about God, and our kids, and about what was yet to be. They helped us find hope and hang onto it.

Without the input of loving fathers, these kinds of situations destroy so many. If you are going through a similar challenge at this moment, I have a word for you. Be encouraged and resolve to yourself that He is good! Joy comes in the morning.

3

Blind Spots and Two-Way Streets

One of the most valuable aspects of a father is their ability to see our blind spots. Blind spots are issues of our character that are evident to others, yet undetected in our own eyes. We all have them! We all get tripped up by them. We all need to realize that we can't always clearly see things in ourselves that others can.

The leadership team in our local church is vigilant to address blind spots. The motivation for this is two-fold: not only do blind spots hurt us individually, but they also have the potential to keep others from coming to know Jesus through us. This commitment to one another has become a facet of our culture, passed onto all the leaders in our body. Recently, I heard Pastor Tim say, "We all have areas in our lives where we are making F's on our report card, and we want those to be A's. Let's work on those together." Are we keeping score, or tallies of one another's failures? Of course not. But we are committed to courageously trusting one another's input, and to growing in Christ.

Courageous leadership requires a willingness to say hard things. Pastor Tim is a great example of this. We have been close for many years, and he has earned the right to say the hardest of things to me because I know his heart. Some of my most painful times in relationship with him have come when I haven't been willing to face a hard truth he was offering me. This happens with people we are fathering, especially in the early stages of our relationship. Whether the issue is a true blind spot or an obvious and known shortcoming, fathers help us identify what will destroy us if left alone.

One practical approach to receiving and applying correction lies in seeking confirmation of the input we receive before committing to a response. For instance, unless I feel strongly that I have heard from the Lord in relation to a correction or prophecy, I will look for confirmation through other people before I take it to heart. If someone says something about my life, I seek out the input of others, being vulnerable and willing to receive from them honestly. (Now, these can't be 'yes' people. They have to be willing to disagree with me, to speak the truth in love, and to offer me truths that I may not enjoy hearing).

Truly Different Than the World?

As we yield to our spiritual fathers and mothers, embracing correction becomes a safe and welcomed occurrence. This process sharpens our character and makes us more effective in His Kingdom. And, it opens a door for others to see Jesus in us. Acts 4:13 tells us that people could identify those who had "been with Jesus," even after Jesus had left the planet! They may not know that He is what they are looking for. So much is at stake as the lost look at the way I live.

What makes me different than those around me? If I live under the impression that a list of "things I don't do" is what will display the glory of God, then I am mistaken. I remember a minister named Larry Randolph saying that he grew up in a church where they sang a song called "This Train." The train in the song was bound for glory (heaven), and he said that they made a list of all the people who wouldn't be on that train. And what criteria did they use? It was all based on their behavior! In his own words, that train was going to be empty because everyone was disqualified. His point was clear: that's not the gospel!

No, it is not the rules we keep that determine our salvation, and much less will they attract the lost to us. Yet we are often told that we need to be different from them to reach them. One remarkable difference that should truly set believers apart is the way we show our love to one another by submitting to authority.

I don't pretend that it is always easy to submit to the leaders in our lives.

Sometimes it is a very subtle rebellion in our lives that our leaders see. We manipulate our situations instead of trusting the Lord to be big in them for us. It seems like nothing, but it is a real form of passive rebellion that keeps us from walking in God's full anointing for our lives. As we read in Song of Solomon 2:15, God is after those "little foxes" because they do indeed spoil the vines. Many Christians live a much-submitted life to God's desires. It is usually not those blatant things that trip them up.

It is usually the seemingly hidden things that put them in bondage, and they begin living a lie instead of the truth God has for them. How can this happen? Slowly over time.

Don't Name the Rocks!

As the story goes, a frog thrown into boiling water immediately jumps out. If the water is heated slowly, the frog will fail to realize what is happening and come to his end. As a cold-blooded animal, the frog is oblivious to the temperature change. We, like those frogs, can be cold-blooded too. The truth is that we can get comfortable with things that have the potential to destroy us. It is like a clever cartoon where a mouse is enjoying a meal, while on the other side of the bushes a cat is watching. The caption for the cartoon is "a false sense of security." Don't we all have things in our lives that could "cook us" like that frog or destroy us like the mouse? Too often, the answer is yes.

Spiritual fathers and mothers are God-sent to show us where we are comfortable, even embracing a false sense of security. Thank God for these people who see what we can't, hope for what we quit hoping for, and love us enough to be brutally honest.

Relationship is a two-way street. Great fathers and mothers are most impactful when they are around people who value their input. In other words, we have to desire to be ultimate sons and daughters as well!

They have to be given an open invitation to speak into our lives. They also need to be made comfortable in doing so. We can make it a chore for them, or the greatest joy and blessing, merely in the way we respond to their input into our lives.

If you are like I was and have become tired of taking awkward trips around the wilderness, this book could be a real blessing to you. That is my hope, of course. Some of my friends and I used to joke about being in the wilderness for so long that we could name the rocks and trees we have circled about so many times. God is so faithful that He will allow us to take as many laps as needed. What I have found, though, is that leaders can help us with where they have been before us.

Lessons Learned from Lessons Learned

In my days as a youth pastor, I would often ask teens this question: "Would you rather go through a minefield with someone who was going through for the first time, or with someone who had been through it many times?" A rhetorical question! Unless we had a death wish, we would all choose the latter. Our fathers have been through many of life's minefields. They can save a lot of heartaches for us and for those who are more hard-headed than others.

Some lessons have to be learned by doing. We probably had to touch a hot stove before we believed or understood why our parents warned us. Some things just have to be experienced. But some don't! If someone tells me that a certain bug bites, I don't have to let one crawl on me to find out. I can take that person's word for it.

I have had to learn through my own mistakes, while also learning from the mistakes of others. The leaders who have most impacted my life have been willing to share their seemingly ultimate blunders. We laugh hysterically when we share our mistakes, and thank God for His grace in teaching us to clean up our messes.

Good leaders will always be willing to lead, but a hallmark of a great leader lies in their willingness also to *be led*. It takes humility to be a good father *and* an ultimate son. We, as sons and daughters, can share ideas with our leaders that they, in turn, use as they father others. I believe that God is always teaching us through those around us. It is ignorant to think that only leaders will have God's heart for His people. But on the other hand, it is equally as ignorant for people to feel they have God's heart completely while ignoring the input of fathers and leaders.

At times, even the most seasoned leaders don't have a clue! But God doesn't tell us to follow and submit to them only when we agree with them. Those are the hardest times, but they can teach us so much if we patiently look for what God is doing. This commitment to fathers and mothers in the Lord can take us to a whole new level.

THE EAGLE

There is a story of a Native American who was watching an eagle in flight. He saw the great bird soar, dip, and soar again.

As he observed the eagle, he witnessed something that would impact his life forever. The eagle forcefully swooped down to the ground and gripped something in his powerful talons. This was nothing new; he had watched the eagle many times before. It is what happened next that became the heart of this man's story told over and over for years to come.

As the eagle soared higher and higher, with its prey in its talons, it began to falter. Suddenly, the bird lost its strength and plummeted to the ground. The man hiked over to the eagle and saw that it was dead.

How could this powerful, majestic king of birds meet such a sudden demise? How could he be soaring high above the world and, in an instant, fall to an unprecedented death? The man reached down cautiously, his question ringing in his mind. As he picked up the eagle, he found the answer. Much to his surprise, the eagle had picked up a weasel for his supper that day. As he soared higher in the sky, the weasel drained every ounce of the eagle's blood. He sucked the life out of him.

Though we may live passionately, do we blindly soar? There are parasites that have attached themselves to us to drain the lifeblood from us, our families, and our ministries. We look for the obvious life-suckers, but a wise father can see the ones that remain hidden. If we are to reach our divine potential, it is crucial that we embrace God's plan for spiritual fathers and mothers in our lives.

4

Father Knows Best

Wonderful! We have made a great first determination. I need fathers in my life to become who God created me to be. I need them because they can see what I cannot see both good and bad. They see what can take me to the next level in my destiny. And they also can see what can keep me from it, or at least delay it.

Lessons from a TV Show

I grew up in the 60s and often watched a television show called "Father Knows Best." It seems like the father in the show didn't always know best, and quite often, just the opposite was true! He was a good learner and learned some lessons quickly from his wife and kids (sounds familiar). Our heavenly Father does know best. He knows exactly who to bring into our lives to mold us and shape us into His perfect design.

Not My Happy Place

Initially, we may not know who God is going to use in this fathering role for us.

I find that God rarely brings people into our lives with whom we tend to agree with all of the time. Those people are seldom going to stretch and grow us because we already think alike. This would be OK, really, if they are willing to hear from God about our lives and refuse to pull any punches.

We can probably expect that it will be someone who has a different personality than us, different methodology, etc. God wants to teach us, challenge us, and stretch us. He will often use leaders to give us a gentle nudge, but other times he uses them to wake us up and move us on. I am so appreciative of the leaders that have been brought into my life! I know that if I need a good talking to, it will be done in love, and I will leave the meeting encouraged and not beat down. Leaders who lead by love always make others feel like they have their best interests in mind. That being said, it can take time for us to feel or recognize their input as love. Trust is a house thoughtfully built; it is not a pop-up tent.

Deposits and Withdrawals

The leaders in my life have poured into me, making 'deposits' of love in so many ways.

When my car needed work, they were there. When my kids needed help with something, they were there. When we were in need, we were not alone. Because of my trust in them, they have permission to make withdrawals from my life because they have consistently deposited into it over the years.

One way they "make a withdrawal" is to share things with me that aren't always easy to receive.

Input like this can be hard to receive unless a father has also deposited much.

Am I a Father to You?

In 1 Corinthians 9:2, Paul says this:

> *"Even though I may not be an apostle to others, surely I am to you! For you are the seal of my apostleship in the Lord."*

I love that Paul states freely that he was not an apostle to everyone. What an important insight for this man to have about himself. He knew his role in the lives of the Corinthian church and intentionally referenced their mutual importance to one another.

Frankly, I will not broadly apply input from just anyone who has a title. A title alone does not equate to true leadership, much less family! It doesn't matter if someone is a great spiritual father to *others*. If they haven't done their part in building a "house of trust" relationship with me, you can bet that I will weigh their input *very carefully*, and especially their correction. Remember what I said about seeking confirmation? Input from someone who does not know you especially well represents a most appropriate occasion to seek confirmation from others.

If the most well-known, dynamic pastor from another church came to me and told me to do something for him, the request would probably be met with resistance. Why would I not submit to a well-known, respected leader? Because he isn't a leader in my life. If one of my fathers told me that this man was going to ask me to do something and my father knew him, then we are talking about a different matter. God doesn't expect us to have blind obedience. But He does expect and require that we follow the fathers in our lives if we want to live out our destiny to the fullest.

We don't require people to "do" anything to attend our church. However, if they want to be involved in ministry, we will have requirements for them. If they desire to serve as leadership in a ministry, then the requirements will be even greater (character and commitment are central). It's OK to just "come to church" – we welcome all. It is not OK to be a leader and live outside of the guidelines of the local church.

GOAT-GETTING 101

The truth is, we don't always welcome fathers and mothers into our lives. Don't worry, our persistent God is willing to use alternate methods to draw us to Him. Sometimes He uses people that just know how to get on our last nerve!

Somebody said that, if you want to get someone's goat, you need to look where they tie it. Sometimes it seems that some people just know where to look to see where we keep our goats. God knows where our sacred cows (goats) are kept and will make sure we address every one of them in due season.

We go through times of not loving as we should. Guess who He sends into our lives? The seemingly unlovable! Argh!

We need more joy. Guess who comes our way? People who seem to rejoice over anything. He knows too well what we need and "whom" we need to make us more like Him.

Three Stooges Revisited

While we continue to examine what it means to be ultimate sons and daughters, keep in mind that God is able to use even difficult relationships to challenge and shape us. He can redeem anything! Graham Cooke is a man of God that has impacted my life greatly. He tells a very poignant story about "three stooges" in his life. (It can be seen on the YouTube video "Throne Room: Three Stooges," which I recommend you watch. It is hilarious and very powerful as well!)

In short, he went through a time in his life where three men made his life, well let's just say interesting. The Lord showed him a vision where three angels were making a very beautiful sculpture. It was simply a work of art! When asked what it was, the Lord told him basically that it was his life. Amazed, Graham asked the Lord who the sculptors were, and when he looked, he couldn't believe his eyes! It was none other than the three men (stooges) who made life so challenging for him during that season. These three were the very men God was using to carve his destiny.

I Think I Know Best

As young leaders, we see "problem people"—those who challenge us in a way that seems unfruitful to us at face value. But God and our fathers see an opportunity for unprecedented growth! Sometimes I have felt that God is blind to something so obvious to me. "God, how can you not see the obvious issues in their life?"

"Laugh out loud," as we say in social media. God does know best who we need in our lives to bring us into the dynamic place He has for us. He also knows the people to bring to us as leaders ourselves that will help carve out the greatness that he purposes for our lives.

He Sees Deeper

Thank God! He looks past the things that are on the surface as He searches much deeper within. God looks at the heart. The key is not just that He sees the heart, but that man looks at the *outward appearance*. It's great that God looks at the heart. It is imperative that we learn to look past the outer shell as He does, to see the wonderful hearts of people. God sees past the outer shell, past what you and I may see initially, and sees the potential of a life lived fully for his purposes and glory. This is the standard that we should hold ourselves to as we consider those lives entrusted to us by Him.

Only the Holy Spirit can help us see what the Father is seeing. And what is he seeing exactly? He sees what the Son died for to redeem back to the Father. How awesome is that! In this sense, God wants us to be blinded to the darkness in others. It doesn't mean we excuse or ignore it. Well, wait a minute. Doesn't it? In fact, they often don't see their faults any more than you or I. They don't realize that they are making a mess of everything they touch. They don't see the people they have hurt along the way. Why would they, especially if they don't know Jesus?

As the Holy Spirit begins to reveal these things, it can be pretty devastating for them. Guilt and shame can overtake them. Fathers can't let what is being revealed keep them from helping those in despair, who need them now more than ever.

Love covers a multitude of sins.

Love doesn't expose; it heals and covers. I know there are those times when it is the most loving thing to do to expose something so it can be healed. But this is not what I am talking about here. I am talking about covering someone who is feeling naked and ashamed.

FATHERING IN, FATHERING THROUGH

It is probably becoming evident to you by now that I am interweaving two aspects of fathering throughout this book. One, of course, is the fathering that we receive, and the other that which happens through us to others. It must be understood that a healthy life is one where fathering is being done to and done through. Simply stated, we will not keep growing unless we are both being fathered and continuing to father others. Think of it this way. What would happen if I continue to grow, allowing the best fathers to speak into my life as I submit to their leadership, but I give nothing out? The answer? Nothing in an ongoing sense. The next generation would be stymied while I grow fat spiritually and probably intellectually. Imagine Michael Phelps, the multi-gold medal Olympian, eating his usual ten thousand calories per day and then not swimming. What if he just sat around after that? It is no different for us feeding spiritually and then doing nothing with that food.

THE NEXT GENERATION

I am haunted by a verse found in Judges Chapter 2. I think we would all agree that Joshua was a very amazing leader.

But look what it says in verse 10:

> *"After that generation died, another generation grew up who did not acknowledge the Lord or remember the mighty things he had done for Israel."*
>
> Judges 2:10 NLT

How could this happen after such a great man of God led the people of Israel? Vision must be transferred to the next generation. The younger generation must begin to carry the vision and walk it out before their fathers are gone.

Ideally, younger generations are walking in God's power and know the mighty works of the Lord. They also have learned to pass it on to their children. This is the formula for success in the Kingdom of God. I don't live my life merely to be my best and enjoy my relationship with God alone. I champion those younger than I and encourage them to run farther and faster than me.

AM I READY TO _____ ?

Recently, I had a thought in prayer that I used in a Facebook blog called "Digging Deeper." We have always asked the question, "Am I ready to go if Jesus came back today?" As I thought deeply on this, here is what shot right through me: "Am I ready to stay if Jesus doesn't come back for a long time?"

Some of the church is so fascinated with the troubles around us that they anticipate a second coming in the near term as a foregone conclusion. The resulting mindset has caused us to fail to build into the next generation, and the next, and the next. "Why should we focus on building, if we won't be here?" D.L. Moody said that it was futile to polish the brass of a sinking ship. After all, it is going down never to be used again. This question has crippled the church, and it demands a valid answer—unless it is the wrong question. The right question, instead, is this: "Why wouldn't we build for even a distant future if there is even the slightest chance that Christ's return is far more distant than we might know?"

The cathedrals of long ago were built to last ages and even took many years to build in some cases. Clearly, their architects were not expecting an imminent return of Christ. It's time for the people of God to start thinking like those master builders. As we do so, we take back the arts, business, government, media, entertainment, etc. We have stood by and watched the world lead so many societal arenas in which God intends His people to flourish. The source of this failure is rooted in a church who is looking to vacate rather than build and advance. No longer can we afford to do so.

"LET THIS SONG BE SUNG FOR A FUTURE GENERATION!"

It is time to stand for those who will come behind us. In Psalm 102:18, we find this cry of David's heart, "Let this be recorded for future generations so that a people not yet born will praise the Lord." That is one of my all-time favorite verses! Unlike the generation in Judges Chapter 2, a people not yet born can praise the Lord if we prepare the way for them!

Our Father knows best indeed. He knows what we need before we ask, and desires to place great people into our lives. He also knows who we need in our lives as leaders that will challenge and grow us as only these fathers can. We must be willing to build and pass the baton to the next generation rather than merely "become fat" at the next generation's expense.

5

THEY HAVE MY BACK

TRUST TAKES TIME AND EFFORT

Open, free relationships with leaders don't happen automatically or overnight. Marcia and I have been married for over 40 years. To hear a newly-wed boast of their faithfulness to their spouse would not impress much. On the other hand, it is a beautiful and powerful accomplishment to be married to one person faithfully for many years. As I stated, it takes time and effort to build a healthy relationship. A marriage takes a lot of work if you want it to be a great one.

It takes similar work if you expect to have healthy relationships with fathers and mothers in your life. Trust is built over time. Husbands and wives are with each other through thick and thin. As the vows say, "in sickness and in health … 'til death do us part." A long marriage will likely be faced with all of the challenges expressed in the vows—some many times over. If they didn't, we wouldn't need these vows!

Adversity either draws relationships together, or it pushes them apart. It all depends on how the tough times are approached. Over the years, we have experienced many trials in our marriage and in the lives of our children. Watching children go through their own battles is very tough for a parent. But, it is also a very crucial part of parenting.

Good spiritual parents know when to be there for us and when to let us find our own way. Good fathers and mothers look for opportunities to show their unconditional love to us. As in a marriage, the true colors of our love are most evident during times of challenge. There is no counting the number of times I have gone to leaders in my life to cry on a shoulder, literally and figuratively.

I have also (figuratively) felt their correcting swat on my backside when I needed it! These times have bonded me with my leaders in such a way that I don't just hope, but rather I know they have my back.

I THINK, OR I KNOW?

If we do not know that our fathers have our best interest in their minds, we simply won't trust them fully. Uncertainties about their motives or commitment to us may cause us to hold back from them. This often takes the form of guarding our hearts, withholding a full measure of vulnerability and transparency in relationships. It can be hard to trust that someone else is so 'for' you that you can let them guard your heart with you, rather than guarding it from and against them.

Several years ago, my pastor came to me with a word of correction that I didn't agree with immediately. OK, I can be vulnerable and more specific than that: my thoughts on the subject were the exact opposite from what he was sensing! Times of challenge and adversity will reflect the measure of trust that I have in a leader. The more this relationship grows, is tested, and proves to bear great fruit in my life, the more I trust the leader. This is such a process and a delicate one at that. Over time, I am able to respond to their input with confidence because they have proven their motive: love. Today, I don't question what they say to me until after I have prayed about it. In other words, my defense rests – at least until after I have sought the Lord. I know that they don't speak to me about my life if it is not important. That is a very safe feeling!

It takes time and circumstance to develop the type of trust that I am sharing about, but we all have to start somewhere. On the one hand, how can we discover whether someone has pure motives if we do not grant them a place of input, to begin with? Love is risky. As relationships take shape, it is proper for the input of a leader to be tested with prayer and counsel. Trust is not built through abandoning common sense. And the more I trust my fathers, the quicker my response to their requests or observations.

I must know that a father or mother in the Lord has my back. This reality causes me to choose wisely whom I allow into my life. I listen to the Holy Spirit about which leaders to be fathered by, the timing of these relationships, and the specific role that Holy Spirit would like them to have in my life. Because someone holds a position of leadership, doesn't mean they are necessarily the one that will personally speak into my life.

Only So Many Eggs

As one of our pastors always says to us, "You and your wife only have so many eggs, and you have to choose which baskets to put them in." Sage advice that has helped us a lot over the years as leaders. I have a limited number of eggs to place in baskets, but I have to make sure how many to place in each one. I need to take more time for some than others. I also need to allow more time for some leaders to place into my basket than others.

Different Leaders for Different Purposes

Sometimes God will use a leader to expose and help with a weakness in my life. Other times God will use a leader to grow and develop a gift or strength I have. If I have a weakness, I probably won't turn to a leader in whom I perceive the same weakness. I don't look to receive financial advice from someone who can't pay their bills. I look for someone who has a proven track record fiscally. I'm sure there is something I can learn from the other person, but I'm not very wise if I choose their counsel in the financial arena! Leaders all have strengths and weaknesses. I can learn from pretty much any leader. God, in His wisdom, will lead us into strategic relationships for unique seasons and needs of life.

TEACHABLE MOMENTS CAN HAPPEN ANYTIME

So, let's get back to our chapter title. 'They have my back' is only realized as I walk with leaders in real life and in real-time. Good leaders will make use of every "teachable moment" possible. What is a teachable moment? Honestly, just about every situation you can imagine can become a moment that a father uses to teach. Isn't that kind of vague? Yes, and intentionally so! Truly the sky is the limit, and especially for growing young leaders. When I say young leaders, please understand that I am not insinuating age. A young leader could be a new believer who is older chronologically. It could be a teen that God is placing in leadership.

A few years ago, Nationwide Insurance had a series of commercials that depicted tough times, saying, "Sometimes life comes at you fast." Man does it ever! Heartache can become a great opportunity for fathering and being fathered. It seems like everything can fall apart at the same time. One of the best lessons I learned from my Pastor, Tim, happened at one such moment.

Tim took the time to illustrate an important concept to me—one that would help me navigate adversity and apply spiritual wisdom to "hard times." The issue was that my car had broken down, and I was upset about it! I just knew that the old devil had chased me down and attacked my vehicle to punish me for my life in Jesus! Tim heard all I had to say about this and reflected that cars breaking down (and other similar, frequent troubles) are usually not the devil. "Life happens," he offered.

Tim shared one of his personal experiences of facing adversity. And he began to share some wisdom that a father had long ago shared with him. We live in a broken world. I had to see that my car was no different. For so many years, I would have responded like this: "My car broke down because the devil is upset with me, and I'm hurting his kingdom." It sounds good (by good I mean spiritual), but the reality is that cars most often break down because…they are cars, and they do that sometimes! Also, they don't always get maintenance as they should. This is a simple example of how input from a father, in a "teachable moment," resulted in a big perspective shift for me.

Fathers recognize these kinds of things and lovingly speak into our lives to show us our blind spots concerning them. In this particular example, the lesson is that we shouldn't give the devil credit for what he didn't do. Similarly, we should resist any temptation to blame God. This is just the type of truth that sons can learn from our fathers. We then can help others who can help others and so on. What have I just described? It's all about Fathers growing sons through real-life circumstances.

Learning From the Masters

Here is another great way to be a father and, in turn, to be a good son. One of my best friends, who is also a dear spiritual father and pastor, is named Harvey Boyd. Harvey has a powerful healing ministry, and people call him seemingly daily from different hospitals to ask him to pray for sick or dying loved ones. Harvey has often invited my wife and me with him to pray for people with cancer and other illnesses. Ultimate sons and daughters will seize every opportunity they get to tag along with their fathers! On these ministry visits with Harvey, we have consistently seen God heal these people. After many years and experiences with Harvey, we are called ourselves to go and see people—with or without our spiritual father.

When he and his wife had gone to Europe on a healing mission trip, my wife and I were called to pray for a man in the hospital who had cancer. It's easy to say intellectually, or as a theological statement, that cancer is no match for the Lord, but we learned this by praying for many cancer patients and seeing Him heal them. Our past experiences of God's power over cancer prepared us to meet with counsel and pray for this man. And guess what? God healed his body, and he has been on fire for the Lord ever since. And this man has a passion for God's healing! He is now a regular partner on international mission trips and in the local church. Amen!

The key to what I just described is, in a sense, on-the-job training. Great leaders look for various ways to spend time with those they are mentoring. Whether taking spiritual sons and daughters along to pray and minister, or simply to help someone move to a new home or apartment, great spiritual parents grab a leader in training and use it as a time to spend with them. As a youth pastor, I loved to take teens from my youth group with me fishing. Hey, it was a captive audience as I saw it. They were in a boat and not going anywhere, ha! It was a perfect venue for pouring truth into their lives.

Recently, my pastor Tim was telling me about a friend of his who was such a great example to him, and also a great example of a spiritual father. Let's call this friend James. One day, Tim asked James what he was going to do that evening. "Motocross riding," answered James. Tim was shocked and commented, "That would be rough!" James explained that he had a spiritual son who was into motocross. James illustrated a powerful truth: he valued his spiritual sons so much that he became interested in the things that his spiritual sons liked to do. Jokingly, he remarked, "I'm just glad the guy wasn't into bull riding!" Like a good natural father, this spiritual father became involved in what his kids like!

Jesus taught His disciples by doing. He then watched them in action, gave them pointers, and ultimately sent them out on their own. He didn't tell them to merely "go" and expect them to assume that all would be well. He was, and is, the ultimate father. Sons with names like John and Peter gave up all to follow Him.

They did well to do so. We don't have Jesus as our spiritual father in the flesh, guiding us, but we have the Holy Spirit and spiritual parents who help us through life. We can follow this pattern as we teach our spiritual sons, watch them minister, and then release them.

WSID (What Should I Do?)

Let me say something that may seem controversial at face value, but may also unload some unnecessary pressure from your inner man: As a son, it should not be my goal to do what Jesus would do in every situation. The WWJD campaign was very well-intentioned, but I believe that it was flawed at its core. Here's why. The movement was founded on the idea that, in every situation, a believer's goal should be to discern and replicate Jesus' actions. (Let me say that I honor those who started and serve in this ministry, and believe that God was honored by it as well!) Despite an awesome motive, I believe that the application point of this ministry became unrealistic and even inaccurate. Jesus gave very general commands like "teach all nations ... heal the sick ... raise the dead ..." Otherwise, He lived by *hearing Father's voice* in every unique moment.

> *"The Father who sent me has commanded me what to say and how to say it."*
>
> John 12:49

As a son, it is my place to hear the Holy Spirit, and to do or say what He wants me to do or say. We are not commanded to try and figure out what Jesus' response would be in the situations we find ourselves. It sounds so right, but we miss the mark totally in doing so. It's the difference between trying to 'do the right thing' in a marriage or remaining actually connected in heart to your spouse.

I am not accountable to doing what Jesus would do, but rather to do what the Holy Spirit is telling me to do. We are free to be led by Holy Spirit, not by a guess at what Jesus would do. An obedient son learns how to hear the Holy Spirit's voice and how to respond to Him. What better way to do this than to spend these kinds of times with fathers and mothers who know the heart of God for our lives? Simply stated, there is seldom a better incubator of growth in our relationship with the Holy Spirit than to spend quality time with spiritual fathers and mothers. Going to movies, going out to eat, going to watch a ball game are opportunities to be relished by sons and daughters who want to soak up all they can from those fathering them.

ALL IN THE FAMILY

God works in and through families in every arena of life. That is why the traditional family is so crucial to the plan of God. God is in a family, and He has placed each of us in them as well. Our churches are families also, where fathers and mothers lead the family of the church. There is no substitute for father and mother time if we want to experience all God has for us! As we submit to their guidance, the blessings of God flow down into our lives and out to others around us.

God built the family and designed it so that everything would flow and function through it. There are no exceptions to this in all of life. People will tell you that I find God in the woods, etc., and I honestly believe they do. But God's fullest expression can only be found in family. He created it that way and, like we said, Father knows best. You can see a blessing on many families even if they are not seeking after the Lord or even know Him for that matter. There are principles of family that bring a blessing just because God ordained it to be so. Why am I sharing so much on family? Because as we assume our role as sons in His Kingdom, fathers will lead us and bring us into the place of blessing and authority that only comes via family. It's really exciting! As society sees fit to work harder and harder to change the family as we have known it, more and more heartache and dysfunctionality will result. Take heart: this will give rise to more opportunities for fathering.

We can't try to change the architecture of God's plan for society without consequences. God is still in control. Our bad choices allow us to taste their fruit and hopefully cause us to desire good choices. We, as a church, have had a real transformation of what this means.

The Gospel, Revisited

Gospel means good news. I truly believe that God is in a good mood, is not mad at us, and has a great plan for our lives. I often think of the gospel in terms of the two trees that God placed in the Garden of Eden.

One was the tree of life, and the other (which they were not to eat from) was the tree of the knowledge of good and evil. Both trees were essential to the full expression of God to Adam and Eve. These two trees are such an important picture of God's value for free will in our lives. Without the second tree and free will, there could be no true life for mankind, because it would not be out of his love and choice that man might choose to serve God.

Let's look at the second tree. It wasn't the tree of knowledge alone. It also was not the tree of the knowledge of evil alone. It was the tree of the knowledge of good and evil. There was good on this tree, and there was bad.

Remember that God doesn't expect me to do what Jesus would do in my situation, but rather only what the Holy Spirit shows me I should do, say, etc. I think we would all agree that it is a good thing to read our Bibles. Some would say that we should read them every day, and not doing so would be a "sin." I'm going to even redefine that word too. Paul makes it very clear that we are dead to "sin."

A few years ago, I had a dream where I came across a bear. It was very unnerving, and I had to think quickly. I tried to get passed it but got caught in its claws. As I tried to free myself from its clutches, I started to feel its teeth cut into me. I had to get free, I thought. So, with everything I had in me, I used all my strength and pulled away. Standing far from the bear I had fought, I looked back to see that I had been wrestling a bearskin rug! That's right—it was a dead bear. I woke up, and immediately heard the Lord say, "This is what my people do with sin. They wrestle with something that should be considered dead to them." Here is the kicker, my friends. That bear was cutting me, beating me up, and destroying me. And it was already dead! If I fight something with teeth and claws, I am going to get hurt, even if it isn't living! That is exactly what happens when we try to "fight" against lists that we call sin.

How often do we find ourselves fighting that which is already dead? We try to "fight" anger, lust, fear, etc., categorizing these as "sin." The word "sin" in the original Greek is the word *hamartia*, which simply means to miss the mark. With the understanding of the Gospel that I hold, I "sin" when I am disobedient to what the Lord is speaking to me about. Sin is choosing to separate myself from him. When I engage in this independent approach to life, I miss the mark that He intended for me, which is intimacy with Him. It always has consequences, or what I like to call "bad fruit."

Back to the Bible, reading again. What if the Holy Spirit tells me not to read my Bible a particular day, but that I should take that time to spend extra intimacy time with Him? If I read the Bible instead, I have just acted independently of Him and, in the truest sense, "sinned." Almost no one believes that this would be sin in this or any other related scenario. Is reading the Bible a sin? Heresy, Pat! I probably would have cried that as well, at one point in my journey. But let's look at this closer.

MAKING A LIST, CHECKING IT A MILLION TIMES?

I spent much of my life with an incorrect understanding of what really constitutes sin. The spirit of religion has created a concept of God in which He is eager and committed to punish us when we step away from Him. I believe that God loves me, is not mad at me, and has no wrath left toward my sin because of the cross of Christ. All God's people say, "Amen!!"

What if I'm in a store, and the Holy Spirit tells me to pray for someone? Most would not say I "sinned" if I didn't do so. But if I understand "sin" to be disobedience, then it takes on a whole new meaning.

I contend that we have been into categorizing "sins" as a list of things that we should not do. But wait, that sounds an awful lot like "the knowledge of good and evil" does it not?

As a result, we have (for example) men everywhere fighting a battle with the "sin" of pornography. Few would disagree that letting our eyes, bodies, and (most importantly) hearts go out toward pornography represents sin. But I believe Jesus calls us to take this all a step further – to realize that pornography is the fruit of independent actions or thoughts somewhere else in that person's life. It's a heart issue.

Man's heart-choice to engage in a life of viewing pornography is the manifestation of a heart that is not turned toward God. Many men miss this point, fighting specific "sin issues" with all their might. The problem is this: when I choose to live independently from God, I don't get to choose where the bad fruit will appear! Let's be clear on this: there will be bad fruit! I would like to borrow an illustration from my friend Matt McMullen and say that life is like a dance in which God is the lead. If I step out of the dance, He isn't mad at me, wanting to punish me. No, He wants me back in the dance (fellowship) with Him again because it is there that I find my life.

You may not agree with this concept of the Gospel's definition of sin, but I must advocate that the freedom from this understanding is indescribable for me! This is good news! It's no longer me vs. a laundry list of sins, each of which requires me to always be "on my guard" and ready to live in a state of warfare. On the contrary, when I am "in the dance" with God and letting Him lead, these issues seem only to become smaller and smaller.

I know that this is only one slice of a large pie that we call the good news. It is key to know what it means to follow the Lord personally, and His plan for my life. When I was shown this, it freed me in so many areas. Sin was redefined—away from a list of things to avoid, and rather as a side effect of broken connection to a loving Father God. A door was opened to walk in a new understanding of obedience and love for my King.

A friend of mine was coming to our church by plane to speak at one of our conferences. As he was reading his Bible, the Holy Spirit told him to put it away. He thought that was a strange idea and dismissed it. He again heard the prompting to put his Bible away. This time he obeyed, and what followed was so powerful! The man sitting next to him engaged him in a dialog that would impact both of their lives. Little did our guest speaker know that he was sitting next to a business executive from a very large corporation! The encounter would have an impact of a special ongoing blessing for his obedience.

We would never think of reading the Bible as "sin," but we don't always pause to consider the heart of God. Without listening to the "now" voice of God, my friend would have missed an opportunity to share the gospel—an opportunity that would only come because the Bible was closed. Wouldn't this have been crushing to the heart of God and my friend too? This is why "sin" can never be about a list we create of pre-approved rights and wrongs.

Sometimes I hear Christians make statements about "cheap grace," lashing out about preachers who do not spend enough of their pulpit time preaching against sin. To entertain their argument, I ask, "What sin should be preached on, and what should not?"

What is the difference between these preachers and the Pharisees and teachers of the law?

The Pharisees of the Bible were men of law and did not have a love for God for the most part. Jesus told them in Matthew 23:15 that they traveled far to find and make a convert, yet made them twice the sons of hell as they were. They were all about the law. They loved being bound by it, and dutifully bound others to it. Yet they were kept from God's love because of their limited understanding of God's true purpose for mankind. We see this concept again in John 5:39, as the Pharisees searched the Scriptures but ultimately missed Jesus.

In 1 Corinthians 1, Paul makes a statement about those who really don't have a heart to experience God. He said that the Jews ask for a sign, and the Greeks seek wisdom.

Did you notice that in Isaiah 7:14, the true sign is prophesied! "A virgin will be with child and bring forth the savior." To ask for a sign, as well-meaning as it might sound, is to ask for something that already is. Paul equates this to seeking power but not realizing that the sign was given, that the Messiah is clearly Jesus, and that He was the embodiment of power.

I don't believe that those who preach against sloppy grace are trying to be like Pharisees. Many ministers are well-meaning, but miss the grace of God out of fear—that their preaching true Good News might not ultimately result in purity and holiness before God. The problem is that claims of "license" are mostly just signs of a lack of understanding of the true heart of the Father. We hear messages like, "You shouldn't drink alcohol, you shouldn't smoke, you shouldn't swear, you shouldn't commit adultery or fornication. Abortion is wrong; homosexuality is wrong." To be clear: I don't disagree with what the Bible labels as evil before the Lord! I only ask, where do you draw the line? Shouldn't we preach against jealousy, anger, lust, obesity, deception, bad health habits, issues of the heart, fear and timidity, greed, offense, wounds people aren't willing to address, and a plethora of others? Again, who decides what this list is? Only God knows the hearts of each person and knows what heart issues need to be addressed that might bring about bad fruit.

I am vehement about this! If I proclaim the all-loving Father-heart of God and teach His goodness and kindness, people will be led to repentance. Romans 2:4 makes it ultimately clear that it is not judgment, but rather the kindness of the Lord that leads to repentance. People don't want to hear about what is messed up about their lives. They want hope and an assurance that they can change. People need to understand the nature of God. He is reaching out to them with open arms right now, right where they are. He is not asking them to take a bath before He can clean them up.

Religion presents a message regarding behavior alone, which is not good news and, therefore, not (by definition) the gospel!

"Itching ears are all that some people preach to" is what some critics of grace say. Paul makes it clear that those who will tickle itching ears at the end of days are not preaching liberty, but rather law. Paul also reminded his readers that they shouldn't use grace as a license to sin. The underlying premise is that our love for Christ compels us to live godly lives. Know this: if Paul was ever to err on one side or the other, I contend that it would be on the side of grace every time!

Paul clearly and repeatedly addresses sloppy grace, but not like many today do. When Paul wrote on the concept of sloppy or cheap grace, he was not looking at it from the viewpoint that it was easy or free grace. Look closely! He was far more concerned with a "gospel" that relies on the law instead of grace. His thoughts on this matter are never clearer than when he asks rhetorically:

> *"You foolish Galatians who bewitched you into thinking that you could start out living in grace and then go back to the law."*
>
> Galatians 3:1

It is clearly the grace of God that frees and enables us. Law can never do this, yet too many teachers still rely on a list of "dos and don'ts" as a means of "protecting" their people instead of teaching them to hear Holy Spirit and give God their whole hearts and desires. Out of fear, many erect fences of law to ensure that they don't stray. This always leads back to death, rather than the precious TREE OF LIFE. The element of choice is cut out of the picture and replaced with a fear-based list of rules.

Fathers Who Understand the Gospel

What does this have to do with being an ultimate son? Everything! Great fathers don't put loads on their sons, which burden and discourage them. Good fathers in my life show that they have my back by teaching me to hear God and follow him. In doing so, they don't try to make me like them, but rather they guide me into being who I am supposed to be by helping me know and hear God in my own journey.

6

THE DEFENSE RESTS

Question: When your actions or words are called into question by another, do you have the usual response pattern? A reflexive, vocal defense? A calm consideration? Perhaps, calling out the shortcomings of the other party in a tit-for-tat fashion?

The "defense" that is referenced in the name of this chapter refers to a defense of our own actions. I want to take some time to explore the process of receiving corrective input from spiritual fathers and offer some insights from my own journey. Being defensive is my way of saying, "I know best." That said, it is crucial to reiterate not only that my Heavenly Father knows best, but that spiritual fathers are "tools" that He intends for my good. Our heavenly Father, of course, is perfect. And we must admit that our spiritual fathers are not. But I must choose to trust their best interests and intentions for my life if I want to grow into maturity in Christ.

SURE, YOU ARE ENTITLED TO YOUR OPINION

Picture this scenario: A father has been praying for a particular one of his spiritual sons and believes that he has received a word of wisdom pertaining to a difficult decision that the son is facing. The father then speaks this wisdom into the life of the spiritual son. That son now has a choice to make – to embrace this input, or to resist it. The son says to himself after the father has offered his words of wisdom, "Well guess what, I can hear God, too. He means well, but I don't need his counsel in this situation! After all, I have the Holy Spirit too. Hey, everyone is entitled to their opinion."

I have portrayed an overtly flawed approach to the input of a father in this brief scenario, but humor me by considering this a bit further. (Consider that we may carry some fragments of these arrogant little reactions inside of us—yes, even us!—even if they're not quite so pronounced.) Could it be that ignoring the wisdom and spiritual fathers keeps us locked in a delusion? Could closing off the input of those ahead of us keep us from moving deeper into the call of God for our life?

If I defend myself, pushing away the input of a spiritual father, I also push away the leader personally. The very leader who has, at the risk of jeopardizing our relationship, been obedient to his sense of leading by pointing out something that I may not see. This has relational consequences, the greatest of which is the possibility of a spiritual father beginning to pull away from speaking into my life. But why would a good spiritual father ever pull away? Good spiritual parents, like our heavenly Father, will honor our free will. And our spiritual parents, also much like our heavenly Father, have emotions which are vulnerable to our feedback. They would never violate or threaten our free will, but neither do they have unlimited time and resources in and of themselves.

I wonder if you can think of relationships that have become strained or distant after wisdom was offered, but not well received. I submit that a mature relationship between sons and fathers should include a process of feedback as input is received.

MY PROCESS

Let me bring this up close and personal. Leaders, in my past, came to me and shared what they felt God wanted to show me and deal with in my life. Again, this is to make me the person I was called to be. Not to make me like them. That is so crucial! We don't need people to make us like them. The goal is always to pursue the person a son was meant to be.

I have a confession to make: many times, as I have built relationships with my fathers, I did not immediately heed their counsel. I validated my actions to myself at the time. And even though I justified my resistance to them in my own mind, I still would fight to understand what their role could be in my life. I had to pray and get God's heart for what the fathers saw. That is the heart of this matter.

Growing in trust toward others is always a process. I feel that I have been on a journey that is "bringing" me to an acceptance of leaders. I have not arrived by any means. There are still some leaders with whom I am growing into that place of full trust, while other relationships happen quite naturally. It isn't as if we come to a place where we just automatically accept all leaders into our lives—nor should it be. Trust needs to be developed before there is an ultimate freedom of expression in a back and forth between fathers and sons.

Leading Means Empowering Others

So, how does this look in real life? Let's say that I have a new leader in my life—in a ministry that I serve in perhaps. I could decide not to be under that leader. That is my choice. However, if I remain, I will have to come under their authority. There is no option. That said, I don't have to make that person a father in my life. They can be over me in a ministry, but I don't have to open myself to allowing them to have full access to speaking into my life. I am 62 years old at the time of this writing, and I have submitted to leaders in their teens or young 20's. In fact, let me bring this a little more up close and personal with two examples I can give you from my own ministry.

First, at one time, I was over the children's ministry in my church. I wrote children's church curriculum, trained teachers, raised up helpers, and coordinated several other items of foundational importance. Over time, different people would step up to serve and lead alongside me, and over me as well. I was on a team with leaders who aren't even (at the time of this writing) with our church any longer. I was under various leaders, led teams, was on teams, raised up other team leaders, and even led our current ministry leader (sounds a little dizzying, no?)

About a year ago, I privately felt that the Lord said that children's ministry would not be a focus for me anymore. I sought the input of my pastor and spiritual father, Tim, and he concurred. Later, as I reflected on all of the different roles I served in our children's ministry, I considered the essence of servant leadership that Jesus modeled. Whether I am personally leading or serving under another leader, I am ultimately serving in the authority system that God ordained. There is not a "more important" role—only different measures of service. We lead by love and are led with His love. If the pastor and elders give a person authority, I must submit to their leadership, regardless of whether they are older or younger than I am.

The second example of this principle of empowering others can be seen in our adult Sunday school community. Years ago, I led the ministry with a team that was beside me. We had one large class that met in the sanctuary. Over time, my team became someone else's team, and then another leader stepped in. I became a support person but remained on the team of that new leader. In fact, he still leads, and I am on his team today.

A few years ago, we decided to add another class that meets in the back of the church. I assumed leadership of that class. The primary emphasis was to raise up new teachers and grow them in their gift. Over time, my daughter joined our team and began to take more of the responsibility of the back classroom. You probably guessed it by now: I handed that leadership role over to her. Now, I am under her and remain on the main team.

It is very easy to feel awkward and miss the role you have grown into, but it is essential in raising up sons to learn to trust the Lord. In this case, I felt His leading to relinquish oversight to my daughter, trusting that God has future, brilliant plans. I am amazed as I watch her grow and take the ministry much farther than her dad did. The same applies to the leader that now is over the whole ministry. He has taken it much farther than I did when I led.

God is so good, and this is just another way He expresses that goodness. It is such an encouragement to watch new, younger leaders blossom into who they are called to be. Sometimes this will not happen unless we step out of the way.

There aren't enough hours in the week to meet with every leader over me regularly, and you may find this to be true as well. But there will often be one or more key fathers and leaders, like Tim, with whom we will meet regularly. With that said, I can still learn much from all leaders in my life and be an ultimate son by serving well and participating in their vision for ministry.

How Does This Play Out?

This is going to look differently in individual situations. People are different, and how they respond to scenarios is going to be different. In fact, the Lord will ask some to respond differently because He doesn't "cookie cut" His children. It might look something like this. Remember, that I am addressing both being a father as well as a son. First, the father or mother would continually be praying and asking God for His heart for that son or daughter. While praying, they may feel God speak to a heart issue, character flaw, selfish ambition, bad fruit, or a number of other things needed to be addressed.

The leader would continue to pray and make sure they fully understand that:

1. God is showing them something—
2. What they are to do with it.
3. If they are to address the son, how it should be done, and very importantly,
4. What is the timing of addressing this?

Remember, when bringing correction to a son, it is crucial to prepare the heart of the son first. How is that done? By praying for them and also asking God to give you (the spiritual father) His heart for them. It is much like a surgeon that uses some kind of anesthetic to prepare the surgery. After praying for them and feeling the leading of the Holy Spirit that it is time, the meeting is set to talk. The father shares his heart, and the son has a decision to make at that point. The son can listen and hear the father's heart and say nothing. This is best! This is where ultimate sonship shows itself. We can hear our leaders and not respond at all, soaking in what has been shared with intention to continue to let God "brood over the waters." We take it to the Lord and ask Him to show us how He feels about what was spoken to us. Where is the truth in this? Is it right? Does the leader see something we don't? How should we respond? Then after settling this in our hearts, we go to the leader and meet again. In my own cases, I have come to the point that I agree with the leader while I'm with them, not defend myself in any way, and discuss actions to correct this. That has been many years of my life to get to this place.

Let me make something very clear here. Sometimes, no matter how prepared, loving, and how much you've prayed, a son will not accept your words. Why? Free will! The power of choice!

"THE WISE MEN'S HALL OF FAME"

Before I went to North Central Bible College (today North Central University) in Minneapolis, I attended a small two-year school in Rice Lake, Wisconsin. It was a very trying time for me as a young believer. I saw God move so mightily during those days, but it wasn't without confusion, temptation, and lots of questions. I decided that it would be a good thing to memorize a number of Bible verses. I went out and bought a green-covered Living Bible. I memorized over 100 verses from that Bible. They became alive in me. They brought me hope, guidance, and power over the temptations of college life. I still have many of them memorized today. One of these verses is Proverbs 15: 31-32:

> *"If you profit from constructive criticism, you will be elected to the wise men's hall of fame. But to reject criticism is to harm yourself and your own best interests."*

I decided criticism was a good thing. Unfortunately, I didn't always heed it. One of the best ways to learn the value of criticism is the pain that comes from it. Pain teaches some very powerful lessons. Very powerful! Have you ever considered that pain is a gift from God? Without pain sensors, we would burn our fingers off and a whole lot worse! Pain can be embraced as a teacher in our lives, as a child learns not ever to touch the hot stove again. It hurts once, but the lesson blesses the child forevermore.

I really don't want to keep familiar with the rocks and trees in the wilderness. If we have a disdain for authority, it will keep us moving in circles. We will think we have vertigo, but we just have issues with authority that have kept our heads spinning. You know those revolving doors where they show people in movies just going round and round? You get the idea. If we don't learn to submit to the leaders in our lives, we may never discover and walk in our destiny.

I used to get such a kick out of teens whom I served as a youth pastor. They would say things like, "I hate my parents! They are so strict! I'm going into the marines." I remember thinking something like, "Hey, we'll see how that works for you." I know that is tough, but God will always bring new authority into our lives in order to help us see what He is teaching us. Some sons and daughters have to come to the end of themselves. In the church, this often presents as a perpetual "hold" on the ministry that we have a vision for. Why? Because the ministry is to *people*. Unfortunately, sons who don't submit will often beat their flock, misrepresenting God's great heart for his people! God is so good. Remember, as we learned in Chapter 2, Father Knows Best!

I wish I would have been elected into the "wise men's hall of fame" a long time ago. I still have my moments of resistance to input from fathers from time to time, even though it is my true heart to receive all that I can from my leaders. *When I know you have my back, I will be open to your heart.* As I mentioned earlier, some sons have to learn by exposing themselves to pain until they say "no more."

While watching the movie "The Great Escape," I learned this truth in action. It was about American prisoners of war in Germany in WWII. They were digging a large tunnel so they could escape. Hence the name of the movie. Charles Bronson was claustrophobic, and as a result, would not go into the tunnel they dug to escape. After many mornings of 3:00 am roll calls and freezing weather, he decided that enough was enough. It was hard for him, but he went into the tunnel and ultimately made his way out. Sometimes, we have to get tired enough of our prison camps and say, "enough is enough!"

I have experienced this type of resistance personally from others. To be clear, there are some leaders who don't foster respect from the people in their ministry. Respect does have to be earned, after all. If I am under someone in ministry, then I am faced with a clear choice: I have to seek God to determine whether I will stay, to honor and serve into the vision of a leader, or whether I will simply leave the ministry. However, I know many people who claim that they can't respect something about a leader – but the deeper issue is nothing more than an excuse to duck authority once again. Hey, the revolving door, remember?

Sometimes God will place us under a leader who doesn't do everything right, who makes lots of mistakes—who is a novice. This is an opportunity for us to learn humility from the Master, even in the discomfort. Leaders are grown by the people they lead, just as people are grown by their leaders. When someone skirts these uncomfortable settings, it is only a matter of time until they will find themselves right back in the same situation. God continues to create scenarios where everyone wins, including ultimately His Kingdom! That is an awesome Father!

7

THE DIFFERENCE BETWEEN "WHY?" AND "HOW HIGH?"

Ultimate sons and daughters cross a threshold in the way that they view authority. When called upon by a leader, our natural response begins with logic. We are taught well to ask, "Why?" Every parent has witnessed that incredible transition in a child's life from pure trust into questioning everything. This happens as they age, as they become "wiser." This occurs around the age of two to three years if I recall correctly from my own parenting experience (Right, son? LOL). The call of sonship, the call to more and more Christ-likeness, is not likened to that of becoming more like a smart adult; on the contrary, it is likened to becoming more childlike. Picture Jesus as he instructs his followers to "let the children come to me …." What is he communicating? The Kingdom of God is just as accessible to children as it is to adults. In fact, Jesus told the disciples they should become more like children if they would like to participate (enter) into the Kingdom!

What's the point of all this? Jesus illustrates that the Kingdom of God is introduced more fully into our experience as we operate from a place of deep trust in relationship—to Him and to each other. So rather than asking "Why?" when a spiritual father or leader asks us to jump (to borrow from an old saying), I contend that a more appropriate and more biblical response would instead be "How high!?"

This requires a level of relationship and trust that most don't realize. Instead of asking, "How high," the quick question/response that we give is, "Why should I jump at all?"

There are only a few leaders in my life that have gained this level of trust with me and to whom I have devoted this level of trust. While only a small number of people have earned my trust at that level, I need to trust more people at a deeper level. There are many people in our lives that have been given authority over us, and yet do we treat them with the level of respect and honor that Jesus calls us to? As I grow in my relationship with the Lord, I should also grow in the level of trust I have with "any" leader that God has given oversight in my life. That is really a slippery slope, some may say! I contend that the real issue is that I don't recognize people in authority as being given that authority by God Himself. Would I question if an angel, or the Lord Himself, appeared to me with a command? I hope not!

The Roman Centurion

The level of faith that Jesus recognized in the Roman centurion was enough to cause Him to take note. It wasn't enough that the centurion understood his own authority. (Surely, that alone would not have impressed Jesus.) What impressed Him was that the centurion equated his authority with exercising faith to see a child healed by Jesus' authority—*in real-time*. That is trusting the authority God alone can give.

Authority is God-given

When I see my authorities in that light, it all changes. Yes, some abuse authority. Some will misuse their authority, and then even rationalize their abuses. I'm a Bible guy, and as much as I have wrestled with this concept, the words just stay there in God's word, challenging me to obedience, and inviting me into the Kingdom. See this passage in Paul's letter to the Romans:

> *"Everyone must submit to governing authorities. For all authority comes from God, and those in positions of authority*

have been placed there by God. So anyone who rebels against authority is rebelling against what God has instituted, and they will be punished. For the authorities do not strike fear in people who are doing right, but in those who are doing wrong. Would you like to live without fear of the authorities? Do what is right, and they will honor you. The authorities are God's servants, sent for your good. But if you are doing wrong, of course you should be afraid, for they have the power to punish you. They are God's servants, sent for the very purpose of punishing those who do what is wrong. So you must submit to them, not only to avoid punishment, but also to keep a clear conscience.

Pay your taxes, too, for these same reasons. For government workers need to be paid. They are serving God in what they do. Give to everyone what you owe them: Pay your taxes and government fees to those who collect them, and give respect and honor to those who are in authority."

Romans 13:1-7 NLT

This is pretty tough to swallow! Paul doesn't mix words at all here. He says that all authority is given by God and that those in "positions" of authority are there through Him. He doesn't even qualify the kind of authority - or anything else for that matter!

ABUSES AND EXCESSES

As I said, we all know there are people who abuse the authority they have been given.

Lines have to be drawn. If a husband is demanding ungodly things from his wife, that husband's authority is not to be heeded. Because there have been abuses and excesses of authority, we are tempted to throw the baby out with the bathwater. We don't say "How high?" when asked to jump because we are uncomfortable with the request made of us. Our discomfort is a great sign that something is God's heart for us. Is it not true that we like to stay comfortable? God likes to stretch us, and often uses leaders who are following a vision that God has given them. Again, there has to be a place for common sense and simple obedience to God.

Recall the words of Peter in Acts 4 and again in Acts 5, when he openly rebutted earthly authority in obedience to God:

> *"But Peter and John answered and said to them, 'Whether it is right in the sight of God to give heed to you rather than to God, you be the judge.'"*
>
> Acts 4:19 NASB

> *"But Peter and the apostles answered, 'We must obey God rather than men.'"*
>
> Acts 5:29

Obedience to God will always be central in our journey into trusting our leaders. We have to grow to a place where we know the Holy Spirit is showing us something is for us or is not.

The World's Craziest Battle Plan

Another great example from the Bible is the story of Jonathan and his armor bearer. In fact, it is the perfect example of not "whether I should jump," but rather "how high." The story is a very familiar one and a favorite for many! It is found in 1 Samuel 14:1-15:

> *"One day Jonathan said to his armor bearer, 'Come on, let's go over to where the Philistines have their outpost.' But Jonathan did not tell his father what he was doing.*
>
> *Meanwhile, Saul and his 600 men were camped on the outskirts of Gibeah, around the pomegranate tree at Migron.*

Among Saul's men was Ahijah the priest, who was wearing the ephod, the priestly vest. Ahijah was the son of Ichabod's brother Ahitub, son of Phinehas, son of Eli, the priest of the Lord who had served at Shiloh. No one realized that Jonathan had left the Israelite camp.

To reach the Philistine outpost, Jonathan had to go down between two rocky cliffs that were called Bozez and Seneh. The cliff on the north was in front of Micmash, and the one on the south was in front of Geba.

'Let's go across to the outpost of those pagans,' Jonathan said to his armor bearer. 'Perhaps the Lord will help us, for nothing can hinder the Lord. He can win a battle whether he has many warriors or only a few!'

'Do what you think is best,' the armor bearer replied. 'I'm with you completely, whatever you decide.'

'All right then,' Jonathan told him. 'We will cross over and let them see us. If they say to us, 'Stay where you are or we'll kill you,' then we will stop and not go up to them. But if they say, 'Come on up and fight,' then we will go up. That will be the Lord's sign that he will help us defeat them.'

When the Philistines saw them coming, they shouted, ' Look! The Hebrews are crawling out of their holes!' Then the men from the outpost shouted to Jonathan, 'Come on up here, and we'll teach you a lesson!' 'Come on, climb right behind me,' Jonathan said to his armor bearer, 'for the Lord will help us defeat them!'

So they climbed up using both hands and feet, and the Philistines fell before Jonathan, and his armor bearer killed those who came behind them. They killed some twenty men in all, and their bodies were scattered over about half an acre. Suddenly, panic broke out in the Philistine army, both in the camp and in the field, including even the outposts and raiding parties. And just then an earthquake struck, and everyone was terrified."

Verse 6 is the most absurd battle plan in the history of the world. Jonathan looks at his armor bearer and utters this incredible battle vision. "Perhaps, God!" That's it! Perhaps God will go before us and win the fight. As illogical and ill-planned as the plan may sound, Jonathan is one-upped by an amazing son! Those are the craziest words. No, they didn't come from Jonathan, but rather his armor bearer. He replies, "I'm with you completely, whatever you decide." Or, as some translations say, "I'm with you heart and soul." What an ultimate son of the Kingdom!

Let's review this battle plan: "Let's go up against 600 men, and our sign of victory will be that they plan to crush us and call us to come up to them." What? Then, in what would appear to be nothing less than a death wish, the plan is to climb up a very steep mountain in full sight of an enemy army preparing their weapons for battle? Put yourself in the shoes of the armor bearer. I think I would have told Jonathan something spiritual-esque like, "Hey let me seek the Lord, and I'll let you know my thoughts." No! The armor bearer very clearly and coherently threw it all on the table and said he was all in! That is what an ultimate son or daughter's heart looks like in relation to the father or mother speaking into their lives. What a beautiful picture! An awesome victory took place!

Is My Money Where My Mouth Is?

Is this easy? No! Recently, I had this tested in my own life. I was working with a team to construct curriculum for our children's ministry. Something I wrote was questioned by a leader, and I confess that I became defensive. Immediately, I felt that aching feeling inside that asked that nagging question of me, "How high?" Ouch!

We are all growing and will find ourselves facing these situations as God tests our hearts and reveals places that need His refining. We have to remember that our obedience to Him is not classically tested by situations that are simplified by everyone's agreement! It will often be situations where we are sure we heard from God about something, only to be challenged by another who believes that they have heard Him. What is incredible with God is that He will often speak something to us, then have the leader in our life challenge it just to see if we trust Him ultimately. "Why would He do that," you may ask? Because God is always after our hearts. He is always showing us what resides in there. Being right is not as important to him as being in right relationship with Him and others in our lives.

A Lesson From a Great Father

I asked Bill Johnson (senior leader of Bethel Church in Redding, CA) a question during a break at a conference one time about a personal revelation the Lord gave me. I was trying to figure out how you help people to see a truth that God shows you. Bill told me that it is more important that people see that you care about them first. Through relationship, truth can be shared. This reminded me of the old saying, "You can't drive a two-ton truck across a one-ton bridge." What a powerful concept to grow into.

What Really Matters

Too often, we are concerned about being right! God is concerned with different things than we are many times. He cares about our love for people. He cares about our servant attitude.

Knowledge, as Paul said, puffs us up with pride. It truly does! Every teacher has had to deal with this as they watch their ministry grow.

Three Huge Keys

I contend that we can grow into a place of comfortably asking "how high" when told to jump. It happens as we develop a combination of keys in our lives. One is trust in the Lord. If I don't trust that He has my best interest, I can't possibly trust that He has men and women in my life that also do. Second, I have to trust that there are leaders who see what I can't see, whom God is giving broader insight into my life. Lastly, I have to allow relationships to grow with those who have any leadership role with me.

Honor the Younger

Learning to submit to younger leaders is a difficult issue for many Christians. As I grow older, and I'm now over 60 years old, more and more leaders are younger than I. In fact, almost all of the leaders in my life are younger than me!

Many are much younger. If we are going to tell people that they are not to look down on those who are younger (see 1 Tim 4:12), then we must model this in our own lives. As we honor those younger than us, we empower them and release the full authority of the Kingdom through them.

There will be more and more younger leaders that God raises up. As I mentioned before, one of the saddest verses in the Bible to me is Judges 2:10. "After Joshua died, a whole generation rose up that didn't know the Lord." The only way to keep that from happening repeatedly is for leaders to raise up young leaders, reproducing themselves for a future generation to walk in power and pass the baton again and again.

Revisiting the Relay Race

Relay races have always fascinated me. Perhaps it is the blend of teamwork with individual responsibility that draws me to these types of events. Have you ever noticed that relays are most often won or lost at the passing of the baton? If I honor and bless younger leaders, they will confidently grab the baton and run quickly and without hindrance.

That is so exciting! But if I don't submit to their leadership in my life, they will stumble and falter as they try to get their grip on the role they find themselves in. I will speak more about honoring leaders in a later chapter. One of the biggest keys to a young leader being successful is who supports them then and along the way. God has such a great plan if we would just embrace it by continually asking "how high" when our leaders say it's time to jump.

Let me end this chapter with these final thoughts about this concept, which is so dear to my heart. I see many young champions-in-the-making who feel that they can reach their potential without entering into a "how high should I jump" relationship. It is so crucial for the local church to create and pass down a culture that truly understands the value of relationships - and the value of people as precious individuals aside from solely their ministry. We all need the hand of fathers and mothers on our lives, guiding us into our personal promised lands.

8

SPIRITUAL ARMOR BEARERS

Let's look closer at Jonathan and his armor bearer. An armor bearer is someone who, among other duties, literally carried the armor of his master. A *spiritual armor bearer* carries a spiritual father or mother before the throne. This is a chapter that will look at how to support your leaders in prayer. We will look at the needs of leaders and some keys to honoring them. I will share several ways that we pray for our leaders and how you can support yours with this extremely valuable tool, or, should I say, weapon? Well, it is both a tool and a weapon. So, let's look at some passages from the Bible and then some other practical items.

> *"I urge you, first of all, to pray for all people. Ask God to help them; intercede on their behalf, and give thanks for them. Pray this way for kings and all who are in authority so that we can live peaceful and quiet lives marked by godliness and dignity."*
>
> 1 Timothy 2:1-2

Let's look at each of these ways that Paul instructs us to pray for our leaders.

1. Pray for God to help them

First, Paul says to ask God to help them. The key to everything in the Christian life is hearing God. How can I know how to pray if I don't hear God? To pray most effectively for my leaders, I have to find out what is on God's heart for them. What is His plan for their lives? What is He speaking to them about? What are they looking to Him for? All of these questions should first be answered directly by our leaders through conversation, and that is a perfectly fine place to start. I also strongly encourage spiritual sons to seek God for more insight into what He is doing in the lives of their fathers. As we pray for them, we begin to learn God's heart for them. We learn to appreciate our leaders more. It just works that way. It's a special intimate thing that develops between us and the Lord as He grows us in praying for our spiritual fathers and mothers.

As I pray for my leaders, I will often receive prophetic words that I am to pray for them about.

In most cases, I share the words with them, and they are very encouraging to them. In other cases, I just keep praying over the words I receive for them and release them if and when the Holy Spirit tells me to.

Every leader I know has the same needs as we do. This is why Paul wants us to pray for leaders as for anyone else. Leaders have families, ministries, jobs, businesses, friends, neighbors, etc. They have crisis moments just like everyone else. Some are weaker than others, and these moments affect them more severely. Others will seem to be unmoved as trials come their way. If you watch the lives of many of my fathers and mothers in the Lord, you just can't tell when they are in a crisis in their lives. But, not all have learned to strengthen themselves in the Lord as David learned to do. Not all have been tested as others have. You will have leaders who are in so many different places in their relationship with the Lord.

You will have very seasoned leaders in your life, and those who are very new to leadership and possibly even to the Lord.

In a previous chapter I mentioned the "Sometimes Life Comes at you Fast" television commercial series. It is so applicable as we grow in becoming "armor bearers" to our leaders. In these times, leaders need God to help them and our prayer support can be so powerful for them.

2. Intercede for them

Paul says to intercede for them. The heart of intercession is to carry someone in prayer before the Lord. The word "intercede" in this passage is the Greek word *entugchano*, which means to have a conference, meeting, or interview. In a sense, the root of this word means to interfere, to get in the way, or intervene. The purpose is to have a conversation (interview) with the Father. God is inviting us to meet with Him (to conference) on behalf of our leaders. Now that is awesome! Paul is saying that we are actually interfering (in a good way) in the lives of people. We care enough to push our way to the throne and to impact change as we receive Holy Spirit's direction for our leaders.

I can't count how many times I've heard people say things like, "I could tell you were praying; I needed your support and could feel it." It is such a powerful reality to know that we can have this Heavenly effect on the lives of those who lead us. Our interviews with God can drastically affect our leaders. I love that!

3. Give thanks for them

Active thankfulness gets our heart in a good place with God in relation to the leaders in our lives. As I become and remain thankful for them, the leaders take on a whole new view in my life. I have heard many say that you need to love someone before you can truly minister to them. I think this really applies to praying for our leaders. As I pray for them and get God's heart for them, I pray for them at a whole new level. I truly am thankful for those God has placed over me throughout my life. I also fully believe that I have become who I am because of them.

I am so thankful for the men and women whom God has placed over me throughout my life. They have often been the mercy and grace of God extended to my life. They help us make the hard decisions if we trust them and allow their input. As I pray for my leaders and get more of an understanding of God's true heart for them, I trust them more and open myself up to their guidance at a greater level.

I am thankful for many things that my leaders represent. I appreciate the safety that their relationship brings, the input into my family and friends, as well as their friendship.

FAVOR!

> *"He has delivered us from such a deadly peril, and he will deliver us again. On him we have set our hope that he will continue to deliver us, as you help us by your prayers. Then many will give thanks on our behalf for the gracious favor granted us in answer to the prayers of many."*
> 2 Corinthians 1:10-11 NIV

The word used here for favor is the Greek word *charisma*. It means "gift" or something that is unmerited. We can bring a new level of the favor of God into our leader's lives as we pray for them. Favor is crucial. We know that Jesus grew in favor with God and also favor with man. That is a huge prayer to pray for our fathers and mothers. "God, increase favor with you and man in my leader's life. Let them see the actual results of this prayer as favor becomes more and more real to them." God alone can give favor, but we can sure be assistants in bringing it.

Favor opens doors, mends broken relationships, and opens new realms of revelation. Favor brings healing, bridges gaps, and closes doors that have long been needing closing. Favor captures the hearts of the cynical and opens the mind to the unimaginable. Favor makes the impossible probable and practical. Favor opens a world that changes the way we view God, one another, and our lost world. Notice I said our lost world. When we gain favor with the lost, we take ownership of reaching those who have not yet been reached.

Favor breaks chains, releases captives, and sets the hardest of hearts free. In Luke, Jesus proclaimed the year of the favor of the Lord. Favor is a non-negotiable for leaders. With it, they walk in anointed, powerful authority; without it, they find themselves living powerlessly.

Favor does things that nothing else can. Favor is what I like to call a game-changer. When I walk into a meeting with an understanding that the favor of God is there, I confidently present what is on my heart and reap the benefits of such favor. It is very powerful that you can be ambassadors of favor in the lives of your beloved fathers and mothers!

My Heart's Posture

In general, prayer and intercession are the lifeblood of any believer. Here are a few other ways that you can pray for your leaders in relation to your life. Now, we will turn to the issue of how we pray and posture ourselves in relation to our leaders.

1. Make my heart tender to their input

I can have the greatest fathers and mothers in my life, but if I don't receive their input into my life, they will serve no purpose to me. My prayer needs to be that I listen with an open heart and value and treasure their input.

2. Show me what I need to learn from their input

I need to be very careful to process what they are telling me and what I need to learn from this. This requires me slowly and methodically going before the Lord and getting His heart about these things. Again, I address the matter of blind spots. Something to the effect of, "Father, show me where I don't see, and help me listen to those who do," should be the center of attention in our prayer regarding our leaders. When I live at this place, I see the blind spots slowly but surely fade away in my life. That is a very exciting time when one or more disappear. Usually, they are lies, and God heals them and exposes them with the truth.

I highly recommend Shawna Burns' book entitled *Seed Digging*. It is a revolutionary book and great guide on the subject of emotional healing. It has changed thousands of children's lives and also many adults! Her website is www.seeddigging.com. I also suggest listening to our podcasts from Grace Fellowship, Cabot, Arkansas, which can be found at www.gfcabot.com. Our services and Sunday school teachings are available—we have two classes each Sunday on different subjects.

3. How do I apply what they input?

I have learned so much about the importance of the practical application regarding leaders' input in my life. There are some big keys to this. It is much like prophetic ministry. What do I do with this? What is the right timing, who else does it involve? These are questions that need to be asked. Pray that you would have these things solidified and implanted in your heart and mind so that you can bless others with the invaluable wisdom you've gained. We shouldn't take these things lightly, and praying about them helps assure this won't happen.

4. Write it down or record it

I know this is a section on prayer, but having prayed about the things spoken into our lives, it is always good to record them in some manner. Going back and listening to (or reading) what leaders have said to us keeps it fresh. It also gives us a great arsenal when ministering to those God has placed under us. On a side note, I highly recommend recording prophetic words spoken over your life!

Prayer Is Powerful!

Prayer for leaders changes the world. It makes them bolder, more on fire, and totally free to share with us and others the heart of God. Prayer sharpens their vision, deepens their passion, and pushes back the attacks of the enemy. Prayer "calls those things that are not as though they were" (Rom 4:17). In other words, prayer shows us God's heart for a leader and calls out of them what does not yet appear to be. That is power, my friends!

9

Honoring and Serving

Blessing What God Blesses

There are many ways to show honor to the leaders God has placed in our lives. One would be living a life worthy of the calling we have received. That, in my opinion, is the greatest honor that I can show a leader! The Bible offers some specific insights on honoring leaders. After we look at these, I will share some of my own thoughts about the subject.

> *"Those who are taught the word of God should provide for their teachers, sharing all good things with them."*
> Galatians 6:6 NLT

This verse illustrates that ministers were paid, even in the earliest churches. Sharing all good things with them implies "contributing" toward their well-being. Sometimes people wonder why someone would give to a ministry that seems to have no lack —or to a minister who seems to have plenty.

The principle of "blessing what God blesses" is powerful. God honors us when we honor those who give their lives for the Kingdom. They may have more than we do. They also have God's favor on their lives, and I have seen the favor of God extended to my life as I bless the lives of those who give theirs for me. We have blessed leaders financially by sharing a meal, giving clothing to them, and even with artwork. God honors the honoring of his leaders. It is that simple! The root of the Greek word for "sharing with" is koinonia, which means to fellowship or to participate with. We honor God when we honor His leaders.

A Culture That Honors

Honor is a key theme in the Kingdom today. God has been showing His people that honor is lacking, and He is graciously addressing this issue to bring blessing to the Church and to the world. It is amazing what this looks like when a culture of honor is developed. My wife received what we believe was a vision from the Lord a few years ago. Here is the vision.

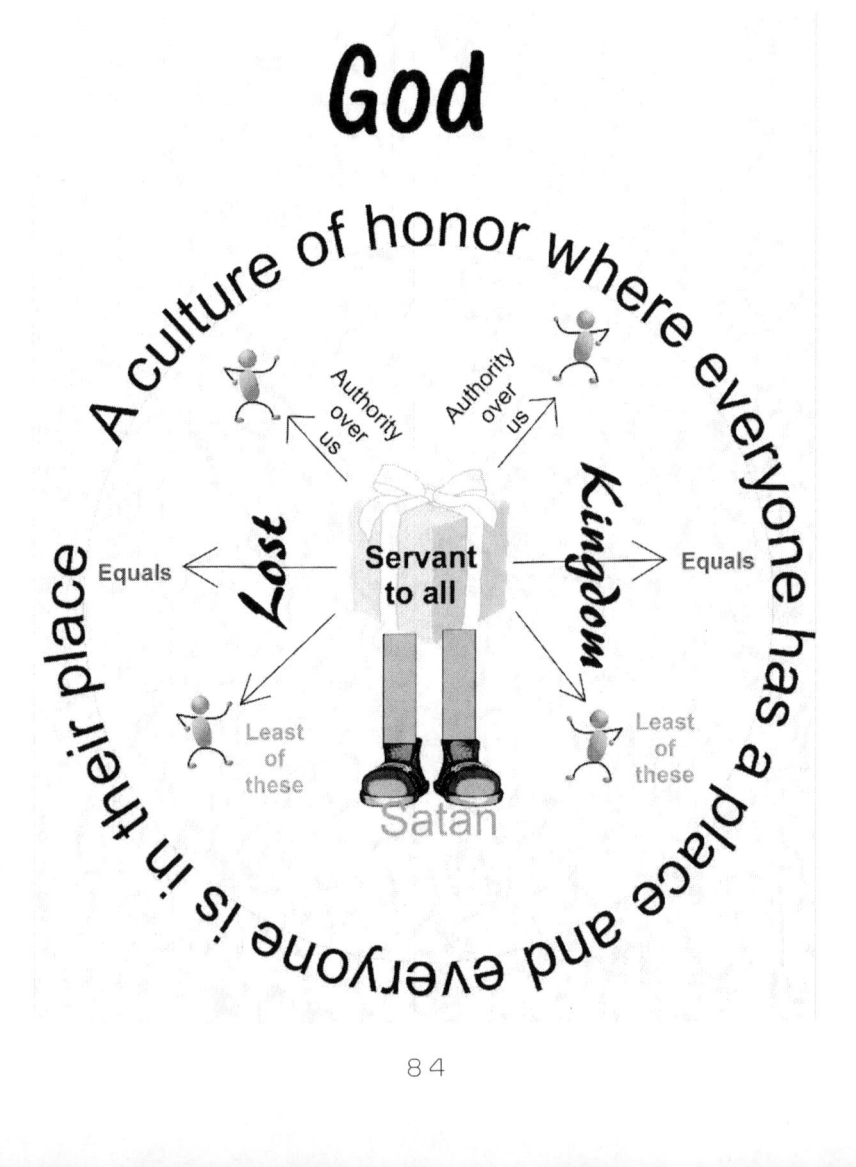

God

A culture of honor where everyone has a place and everyone is in their place

- Authority over us
- Equals
- Lost / Kingdom
- Servant to all
- Least of these

Satan

THREE LEVELS OF SERVICE

One who serves is a gift to all. To both the Kingdom and to the world, a servant is a blessing. My wife's vision highlights three 'levels' of service.

1. THE LEAST OF THESE

These people are those whom most of the world ignores, neglects, and turns away from. Shouldn't this happen less in the Kingdom than in the world? Unfortunately, the glaring reality is that the Kingdom of God has far too much favoritism and far too many cliques. Our divisions lead to the neglect and avoidance of the "least of these." The world consistently shuns the least of these in the workplace, and anywhere else they may be found. I feel the heart of the Father is to see this change as His Kingdom impacts the attitudes and cultures of the Church and the world.

I love the way that my pastors lead our local church to cherish people who God loves so much. The mentally and physically handicapped, the poor, the homeless, the eccentric, and others are regularly embraced in our fellowship. Jesus says that when we love these people, we are actually loving Him.

Our church will often find creative ways to live out expressions of love to the neglected. One of my favorites is a Christmas tradition that we call "Project Give." One year, an assignment was to give a gift card to a stranger. My wife and I blessed a waitress who was expecting a child, and later a young Salvation Army bell ringer. We were touched by their responses – smiles, tears, and the sentiment that they had never had anything like this happen to them—priceless! My wife printed on the cards that they were from Jesus' family. We told them they mattered to God, and He cared so much about them. I trust they felt that care and love at least this one time. It was a perfect opportunity to bring the Kingdom to the least of these. That is a culture of honor in a community!

2. Peers

Our peers are the people we work with, serve with, minister with, and such. Peers can relate to one another on so many levels. We have many of the same challenges and have what some would consider to be the same common enemy.

I used to do seminars with seniors as part of my job, and I would often tell a joke. It goes like this: Why do grandchildren and grandparents get along so well? The answer is that they have the same common enemy. You know, the parent of the child is the child of the grandparent. (We all know that they aren't really enemies, but it makes for a good joke around the seniors I mentioned.) Of course, our bosses and leaders aren't our enemies either, but many times they are viewed in such a light. Our coworkers have the same people who are over them. Some at least. You get my point: We are equals with others because of factors that create that commonality.

What often makes Christians uniquely stand out is their willingness to honor and follow the leading of the authorities in their lives. The church has too often missed the mark by thinking that seemingly worldly issues don't matter, or, at least, they don't matter as much as spiritual ones. We can display and highlight the reality of God's Kingdom at work, at the pool, or in a restaurant.

When I willingly serve the leaders in my life, I shine a beacon on Jesus that the world can't ignore. Often, our culture is interested in submitting to leadership only to the extent that those in submission ultimately benefit. There seems always to be an end-game that provides a foundation to worldly honor systems: promotion, upward mobility, reputation, or money. This is not God's culture of honor, and can't be the case for believers. Whether at work, at home, in the marketplace, or in church, we have such an amazing opportunity before us to show the world how we are different.

3. Those over us

This brings us to the third level of service in my wife's vision: those who are in a role of authority, both in the world and in the Kingdom. Let me, at this point, say something that is crucial. Wherever I find myself, I am in the Kingdom. "Sacred" and "secular" are no longer divorced from one another. The Kingdom of God is the rule and reign of God, and Jesus teaches clearly that it is in us! Let me be clear, if not redundant: if the Kingdom of God is going to come at your work, it is not going to come "down," or "around," or in some other ethereal sense. If it is to come at all, it is going to come through YOU. As the Kingdom flows from us, we bring each place that our feet tread under the realm and influence of the Kingdom, whether we are aware of it or not.

Leaders, rulers, and authorities of various kinds are all placed by the Lord. In perhaps a frightening (but clearly Biblical) reality, He chooses and uses some of the most vile, godless, cruel men and women at times. More and more believers are welcoming this reality and are no longer looking for a job with a "Christian boss" and a great "Christian environment." If that is where God has placed you, great! But, the key is being where God wants us to be. Period! We have the privilege of changing an atmosphere with our presence. This reality makes my heart sing, and I know it makes His sing too. It is why He made us. He made us to re-present Him. To build, expand, and further His Kingdom. Our greatest opportunity on earth is to re-present our good Heavenly Father to so many who view Him as angry, punishing, and never fully satisfied or pleased. What an honor!

Who is My Teacher?

We began this journey into the concept of honor with an important scripture. Let's go back there now.

> *"Those who are taught the word of God should provide for their teachers, sharing all good things with them."*
> Galatians 6:6 NLT

A teacher in this verse is not a teacher only in the strictest sense. It is anyone who brings instruction into your life. The Greek word for "teacher" used here is *katekesis*, and it refers broadly to anyone who communicates instruction. This is not the Bible's main word for teacher, which is *didaskolos*. Instead, the word Paul uses in Galatians 6:6 is less formal.

Why do I take the time to make this distinction? There are so many people in my life who have brought light and guidance to me, and yet many of these would not be initially considered as "teachers." In fact, they would tell you themselves that they are not teachers at all—at least, not in that strictest sense of the word. In too many circles, the only recognized or valued teaching is that which takes place from a pulpit or a Sunday School classroom somewhere. I have no interest in downplaying this formal and central role of teaching. But because of Paul's choice of words, we must recognize that there is more to "teaching" than preaching. We would be wise to recognize and honor those who speak into our lives.

MOVING FORWARD IN HONOR

Looking at the concept of bringing honor to those who instruct, I offer these challenges. Ask yourself these questions and apply them in your life. How can I financially bless those who instruct me? How can I encourage them with words? How can I thank them and invite their input further? What can I do to serve them and make their lives easier and more productive?

Ultimate Sons and Daughters Lay it Down

I encourage you to seek the Lord on ways to serve leaders in your life specifically. One of the best ways is also the simplest: just to go to a leader and ask them how you can serve them. "What would make your life easier? How can I lay down my life to make you more successful in the Kingdom?" This is a question that ultimate sons and daughters never stop asking. Listen closely to the responses they give. Realize that you may have to dig a little to get to the heart of what matters to them, especially if they are a very humble leader.

Great leaders are always asking their people to share "big things" that are in their hearts. Ultimate sons and daughters will respond by asking leaders about seemingly "small things" that will bless the leader. Serving leaders can be very practical. Serve their family in any aspect you can. If it is a male leader, it is crucial that the wife is honored and not left out. Too often, the spouse of a leader finds themselves left on the outside of receiving service and honor. Other details like cleaning offices, vehicles, and other related items, can be blessings. Maybe they have young children or grandchildren who you could babysit so they can have a night out. Watch for menial tasks that the leaders are doing.

What can I do that would be a relief to them? Things like cleaning around the church, setting up and taking down tables and chairs, and passing out papers are common tasks that we can all help with. What ministries are they over that you could help serve? How do they serve other leaders? Great pastors and leaders are servants. The servant is the greatest, according to Jesus! The bottom line to serving leaders is to insert yourself into their life in a place of honor and service, asking them and also asking God for ways to bless. Then serve and honor with your whole heart and watch the fruit come out of it!

10

Learner vs. Teacher

A teacher can only teach if a student lets them. When I meet with a "teacher" in my life, I must realize that it is not time for me to teach, even though I am a teacher! It is time for me to learn and maybe occasionally add some insight.

Scripture offers us multiple pictures of father/son relationships, in both Old and New Testaments. The successful ones have a common thread: a son knows how to humble himself to receive all he can. As I said before, when a student is ready, a teacher can appear.

Moses and Joshua: A Great Father and a Great Son!

Moses is one of the earliest examples of a spiritual father, and Joshua learned much from him—enough to lead a nation. Imagine a scenario in which Joshua was preparing all of his wisdom to teach Moses what was really important. Finally! Wait, no, that is hard to imagine. Joshua had a very clear passion for the Lord and an uncanny heart of courage and leadership. Can't we at least assume that there were some revelations that he received from the Lord that would impact Moses' life? Consider the wisdom that flows out of the book of Joshua! But how might the book of Joshua look today if he had spent his time trying to teach Moses instead of learning from him?

I contend that much of what we see in the book of Joshua was inspired in Joshua through his father, Moses. God clearly spoke powerful things to Moses!—the recipient of the main ten laws. This man, Moses, spoke with God face to face. He wrote several books of the Bible; Joshua wrote one. I don't think that was a coincidence. Moses desired the presence of God more than anything. It would be logical to surmise that many of the one-on-one lessons between Moses and Joshua were discussions about hungering for God's presence. I can't prove that, but I know that people reproduce their passions in others. Joshua learned what he did, and became who he was, thanks to his heart that hungered to glean from a father's vast storehouse of wisdom and knowledge.

ELIJAH AND ELISHA

This is clearly one of the most powerful pictures of mentor and student in the Bible. Elisha recognized the anointing in Elijah's life and wanted more. His hunger and diligence would ultimately pay off. Like Joshua, who took up the mantle of Moses' leadership, Elisha would one day see a double portion of Elijah's anointing on his own life.

ALL IN!

What impacted Elisha so much that he would be "all in" as a disciple of Elijah? Elijah was not your typical Israelite, and Elisha knew this full well. Elijah's passion for the Lord was powerfully demonstrated as he walked out the call on his life. How many other people did Elisha witness who equaled Elijah in his authority, his zeal, his power? Who else was performing the kind and number of miracles that Elijah did? The answer would be um, none! Elijah raised the dead, faced off against false prophets, did some of the most unusual miracles, and impacted kings! We don't know all Elisha saw in Elijah, but we see this clearly: Elisha would give his all to follow his new mentor.

When he met Elijah, Elisha was plowing with his oxen in the field. Let's look at the story in the Bible.

"So Elijah went and found Elisha, son of Shaphat, plowing a field. There were twelve teams of oxen in the field, and Elisha was plowing with the twelfth team. Elijah went over to him and threw his cloak across his shoulders and then walked away. Elisha left the oxen standing there, ran after Elijah, and said to him, 'First let me go and kiss my father and mother good-bye, and then I will go with you!' Elijah replied, 'Go on back, but think about what I have done to you.'

So Elisha returned to his oxen and slaughtered them. He used the wood from the plow to build a fire to roast their flesh. He passed around the meat to the townspeople, and they all ate. Then he went with Elijah as his assistant."

1 Kings 19:19-21

What significance is found in the way that Elisha made this transition! He could have left all of his "past" in place, and simply followed by leaving intact the things of his occupation. He could have burned the plows and kept the oxen. He could have simply purchased new plows. After all, he was from a family of means. No. He slaughtered the oxen, burned the plows, and then fed the townspeople with the meat. There was no thought of turning back.

No Turning Back

Elisha realized that when Elijah threw his mantle over him, he was being given an unbelievable call by God. It wasn't Elijah that was calling him, but rather the Lord Himself. That was huge! In his mind, it would require leaving all and running hard after Elijah.

This was an opportunity, as well as a calling for him. Would it be possible for Elisha to step into this calling without immediately following Elijah? Probably so, but with a cost. The cost is the same for each of us when we ignore or minimize the importance of our fathers in our lives. They simply know what we don't, have experienced what we haven't, and have been to places in the spirit that we only can imagine at this point. It wasn't a convenient time in many ways for Elisha to leave it all to follow Elijah. He had a career and had a lot to lose from an economic standpoint. He loved his parents and didn't want to leave them in the dark as to his plans and even whereabouts. But, he knew that he had to move quickly. Sometimes we have to make sacrifices to position ourselves to tap into the wealth that our fathers and mothers bring us.

One of my own areas of personal, however small, sacrifice has meant meeting early or late with my fathers. It has often meant meeting with them when I probably would least like to. For instance, I will occasionally search out road trips, and car rides with one of my fathers to take advantage of the times that would not otherwise be afforded to me. When you recognize how valuable they are, you make sacrifices to be with them and spend time with them.

Double Portion

What was the result with Elisha and Elijah? He received a double portion of Elijah's anointing. Elisha did twice as many miracles as did Elijah! Elisha actually became the prophet that anointed Jehu, who killed Jezebel, who was a constant thorn in Elijah's side. She caused him to cower and flee for his life. Maybe hearing the story of Elijah and Jezebel gave Elisha even greater resolve not to be another victim of Jezebel's control and schemes.

One of the most beautiful things we see in this father/son or mother/daughter dynamic is a pattern by which a disciple goes beyond the mentor in some ways. For example, I may see weaknesses in my leaders that I can learn from. I may see the Jezebel that they can't slay, and yet I am able to. I may see a flaw in a leader that I can turn into a strength in my leadership of others.

I will certainly see my own weaknesses that need to be recognized—little foxes that can spoil the vines. They are the seemingly "little things" that can destroy any ministry by destroying the minister. Elisha had a keen sense about this and wasn't going to miss the opportunity of maximizing his training to be a prophet. He knew that if he didn't jump on this that something would be lost. Of many things he learned from his father, Elijah, this would be one thing he needed that would transform a specific situation he would encounter. He did well as a student to learn from his teacher, and this equipped him to face all that would come.

To the High-Dive for Elisha

Elisha felt a call to Kingdom greatness and was going to dive headlong into it. He wasn't going to dip his toes into the water; he was going right for the high dive. But did he really do that? Elijah graciously allowed Elisha to walk slowly into this calling with nothing to fear. But that wasn't the approach that Elisha was taking. He was going for broke and at all costs.

Not only did Elisha learn from Elijah's weaknesses, but I think he was also inspired by them to greatness. When fear hit him in regard to Jezebel, Elisha could stare it in the face and boldly say, "Not on my watch! I know what you did to my spiritual father, and I am not going to let you do that to me now." I can only imagine the resolve that Elisha carried under the mantle of his father, Elijah. Like him, we can learn from our leaders' weaknesses and simultaneously be inspired to break through the barriers that they could not.

Impartations

New and greater anointings are constantly being released in the Kingdom from one leader to another. I believe that these anointings are created when we become hungry for more. We won't quit! We won't give in to the challenges that face us!

We learn from our leaders' shortcomings. We are inspired by them, and garner a passion inside us to find an anointing that breaks those chains once and for all for us, our families, and our spiritual children. The cost of walking in our fullness may be great, but the cost of missing our potential is so much greater! Too many will be hurt if we don't pay the price. The loss to our loved ones is much greater than the cost of embracing the pain and pressure to become who we are called to be in the Kingdom.

The Ultimate Spiritual Father

There is no truer model or picture of the ultimate mentor than Jesus Himself. There are numerous men and women who would never be the same because of His fathering. He was and always will be the ultimate father because He always listened to His heavenly father. To be a great mentor, we have to hear God for the people we are growing. The disciples, Mary, centurions, Jewish leaders, and others, were impacted by the life of this "simple carpenter." Like great fathers in my life, Jesus could guide and correct people with a good heart and always encourage them to see the value inside of themselves. Even when my fathers correct me, I walk away from those times lifted up and encouraged. That is fruit that should always be a part of a healthy relationship with a father.

There are multiple examples of mentoring relationships in the New Testament. Paul and Timothy, Barnabas and John Mark. Paul found little patience with dealing with Mark, but Barnabas "The Son of Encouragement" never gave up on this young warrior. He saw great things in him! At one point, Paul and Barnabas had a falling out over this young man. Even with the great anointing and passion that Paul had, it was Barnabas who could see past the young John Mark's inexperienced, compulsive nature.

It reminds me of one of my most memorable illustrations from one of my favorite Bible college professors. He had many great ones, but this is one that really impacted me and has stuck with me over the years. This precious man has gone on to be with the Lord more than 35 years ago. He was illustrating how God's goodness and mercy pursue us, as stated in the 23rd Psalm. He told us of one of his many hunting adventures. He and his friend were pheasant hunting, and he had a new hunting dog he had been training.

They shot a pheasant, and his dog was off to the races. He watched as his new hunter chased after a downed pheasant that was injured but could still run. The pheasant turned a sharp corner in the cornfield, and as it did, the young dog turned too fast and rolled through the rows, narrowly missing its catch. My professor watched as his friend's older, more mature dog turned the corner. With great finesse and patience, the more seasoned hunting dog ran down the pheasant.

He reflected that this was a perfect picture of God's goodness and mercy following us all the days of our life. There is also a lesson here of a father seeing past only the exterior of the young, immature leader they are raising up. My professor didn't get rid of his dog because he made a mistake! He didn't give up on him with his first negative experience. True fathers see the potential of the younger and know how to draw it out of their young sons and daughters. I have painful memories as a young leader when those who could have been great mentors failed to see the value of being patient with growing me. It was easier to discard me than to help me through my weaknesses to see the greatness in my life. Barnabas did this with young Mark.

11

The Leader's Picture

The Bigger Picture

It is crucial that we understand God's heart for mentoring! We have to realize that He gives leaders insight into the lives of those they are fathering. In our church, we call it seeing pages (or chapters) ahead in someone's life. If God brought a leader into our lives, we have to believe He also is going to give insight to that leader for our process with God. That is just God's nature. How could a father grow a young leader if they didn't see anything more in their life than the young son saw in themselves already? It isn't a bad thing to walk in a mutual, side-by-side relationship with someone. But to truly impact a life, a deeper insight into that life is imperative.

Account-ability

I've heard Bill Johnson say that accountability is not about keeping people from doing bad things. We have given accountability only a negative connotation. "I am going to keep you accountable" has come to mean that I am going to keep you out of trouble. I am going to help you not "go back" to your past, your vices, etc. It is all about looking at the dirt and trying to avoid it. The mainstream idea surrounding accountability is all about building a wall of protection that keeps someone from being like a pig that goes back and rolls in the mud. But the heart of accountability is really about something else. It truly is about "accounting for one's ability." It is about calling out greatness in people where all most can see is a crusty, dirty exterior.

A Lot of Dirt

There is gold in the dirt. But sometimes there can sure be a whole lot of dirt! In a younger or less mature son, we should expect that a greater amount of "dirt" will be ours to sift as we look to find the gold. In a mature son, more dirt has already been sifted through over the years. Have you also noticed that someone who has been a Christian for decades can also have a tremendous need to shovel away old, stale dirt?

Our job is to find the gold and look past the dirt. More accurately, our job is to see the dirt, recognizing that it is very real, and to look past it by calling out greatness in our son's and daughter's lives. Why does a gold prospector painstakingly go through pounds or even tons of dirt? They are totally convinced that under the dirt is a vein of gold—not just a nugget here and there—but a vein. If we treated those whom God has placed in our lives in the same manner that a prospector approaches his or her potential gold mine, we would see far more people reach their God-given destiny.

A Christmas Story

I apologize in advance for the nature of this next illustration, but it is so fitting that I could not leave it out. The story goes like this: a young boy was not being the best example of the perfect child, and Christmas was on its way. His "Christmas list" was long, but he was not obeying his parents. He was beating up his siblings, and just making life rough for mom and dad. Dad decided that this year would be the time to teach his son an important lesson about how obedience works, a lesson he would never forget. He did something dramatic: he took a box and filled it with manure. Stay with me—I know this is gross, but it does make a very good point.

As Christmas drew closer, the boy's anticipation grew with each day that passed. Then Christmas morning arrived. There, in the front room, was a large box of manure with the boy's name on it. When it was time, he tore open the box and, to his surprise, found the strange contents inside. But to the shock of his parents, he began to reach into the manure and feel around. The parents, in awe, asked what he was doing. He exclaimed excitedly, "With this much manure in here, there has to be a pony somewhere."

What was in the heart of the little boy, this immature child, as he processed what he was receiving on Christmas morning? Was he "connecting the dots" between the strange gift and his own behavior, which led to the gift? This little guy must have been thinking that he was being a brat lately, but his parents loved him so much that they still wanted to bless him. He expected a pony, after all!

We have to view our spiritual sons and daughters in the same way. With all the junk and baggage, etc., there is a treasure in there somewhere for us to find. No matter how bad it seems, we will just trust Him and not give up on them.

Looking Past the Obvious

Hopefully, you can get that last story out of your minds now. If I was on my phone texting right now, I would no doubt expect a good LOL. To bring this back to focus, great fathers and mothers know how to see past what everyone else sees and look to the heart. Actually, they *learn* how to do this.

Sometimes there is a temptation only to see the exterior and miss the treasure beneath. I mean, how much bad stuff can one person have in their life? It is crucial that we stop asking that "external" question and focus on a much bigger one. That question would be, "How much gifting and anointing lies past the gross, glaringly obvious shell?" It is in doing so that we begin to see true greatness and step into the opportunity to call it out. It is only in this way that a person's full potential is realized for their life. How would Gideon or David have fared if they had not been confronted with God's ideas for their life? Would we even know their names?

In general, most people consider themselves as failures: not good enough, not attractive enough, not well-spoken, not world-changers, too messed up, and not worthy of love. This is all interrupted by a father who sees the bigger picture. If your spiritual child sees himself as unlovable, then love them extra well! Demonstrate the love that can only come from the Father and can only be realized when in right relationship with Him. He is the only one that can help us love well, and love in a way that captures a heart that doesn't know or understand His great love.

A son who carries "not good enough" needs to be shown that his worth does not come from what he does, but rather who he is—who God says he is! Too often, people place their sense of value on performance. When this is the case, no one is good enough. There is always more that could be done, could be done better, etc.

Beneath very real outer dirt that has to be dug up, you will find treasure. Greatness is there. Unique destiny lies just below! What a great banner that would make! If we could just help people to see this about their lives, they could walk around knowing that just below my ugly, crusty, immature exterior lies a treasure and manifest destiny. Can you imagine a whole community of people who think and live this way? Guess what, God can! It is His ultimate plan for every one of us to know and understand our purpose and the plan He has for us.

Purposeful Recalculating

It would be great if every time we went the wrong direction or made a mistake, we could have a life GPS that would boldly announce to us, "Recalculating!" "You went the wrong way. When possible, make a U-turn and get back on track." Well, actually, God did make such a device in a way when He called fathers into our lives. They see when we need to be "recalculated" and placed back on the right path, so to speak.

We go through life, and, at times, we turn right when we should have turned left. Or we turn left where we should have gone straight. Whew! That sets the groundwork for a messed-up direction for our lives. However, God is so gracious that He accounts for our mistakes and brings people to us who can help us understand our mistakes. He wants us to have relationships that keep us from making the same wrong turn over and over. Even if we are far from the destiny that God purposed for our lives, we can be "recalculated" so that a directional turn begins to take place.

Many feel they are beyond hope, but God never feels that way about anyone. Nowhere does it say in the Bible, "He who began a good work in you says, I give up." It says instead in Philippians 1:6:

"And I am certain that God, who began the good work within you, will continue his work until it is finally finished on the day when Christ Jesus returns."

God is working in our lives, and will not stop until He has completed the work He intended. We are special! We are unique! We are invaluable to His plan and purpose in building His Kingdom! If those are all true statements (and I fully believe they are), then the world can't afford for us to believe any different about ourselves.

All of creation is crying out for the manifestation of the sons of God. The whole earth is massively impacted by the sons of God becoming "the sons of God." Fathers play one of the most key parts in this. Without fathers, we might achieve even some level of greatness in our lives, but not the full extent that the Father desires and has purposed.

How does this progression look over time? We begin to believe a lie about ourselves even as a very young child. It is then compounded by other events in life. Trauma is multiplied. We begin sabotaging relationships. One lie gets stacked on top of another until we have layers of things that we believe about ourselves that just aren't true. And, not only are they not true, they are far from what God feels about us. It's like driving a car with a windshield that is covered in mud. The windshield wipers try to clear it away, but it is too thick. In this scenario, a driver will find himself in many possible outcomes. None of which is ideal! We face life the same way. We end up in ditches, go off the path, run into and hurt others, and a host of other negative results due to the lies we've believed.

Once again, I must recommend the great book *Seed Digging* by Shawna Burns. Her book is found at *www.seeddigging.com*.

The Answer?

The answer is to welcome fathers and mothers into our lives. With them, we invite God's true heart toward us. If there is not someone in your life who speaks strong things to you like: "That's not God's heart for you; you are believing a lie in that area. You are so much more important than you realize. You are unique and have such a purpose. You can't get into your destiny with ____ in your life." Maybe it's time to look for a father or mother. Ask God to send you great mentors. Then look for them, welcome them, and open your life to them.

Over time, you will see the lies erode as the great truths of God for your life unfold. The dirt will be sifted, and the deepest treasure will begin to emerge. God is faithful, and He will reveal the treasure to your spiritual parents. As you believe more of the truth God has for you, you become more confident in living who you were meant to be. What now becomes natural is living in your destiny, rather than living in shame, condemnation, embarrassment, and self-degradation. Life becomes a new series of good choices, and the bad choices are few and far between.

It doesn't take place overnight, usually (there are rare exceptions), but it does evolve. Change usually takes time to occur, because it wasn't overnight that bad choices turned into a life of bad fruit.

But the great news is that, as the right choices are made, and the corrections take place, good fruit quickly follows. Now that is some really good news! In fact, that is the heart of the gospel. It isn't the mad dad that can't wait to punish a wayward child. It is a happy father who feels pain rather than anger when we need "recalculation" in our lives.

Good parents feel much worse for the child who disobeys than they do for themselves. It breaks God's heart when we don't live our lives in the understanding of who He intended us to be. It doesn't anger Him. As spiritual parents, we have to be careful that our children's mistakes and mishaps don't distract us from seeing the gold that lies within.

Our spiritual children need to know that we believe in them, are there for them, and that we are not going anywhere. As spiritual children ourselves, we need to humble ourselves and keep that door open to those speaking into our lives. If we don't, we can be assured that the lies will resurface, and so will the bad fruit we've known so well.

12

Where Do We Go from Here?

No Greater Honor

Leaders are never more honored than when they see you and me fathering others with the gems we received from them. That is what fathering is all about! God brings people into our lives who father us, and then He brings people into our lives for us to father. It is an ongoing cycle of family.

Like Fathers, Like Sons

As spiritual families develop, entire groups of people will take on the mannerisms and characteristics of a father. Sometimes it is even comical to watch this play out. Tim is a great example of this. When I first met him, he was in the habit of praying a certain way. Soon, everyone whom he was fathering would start their prayers with the same words. Some others mimicked his worship style. I don't know if they do it on purpose or not, but it happens! The influence of a life well-lived is very powerful and contagious.

Great spiritual fathers and mothers will have many walking in their footsteps, and you will begin to notice when a great family is being established. This is how culture is formed: influence is carried from generation to generation, affecting dialect, art, behavior, and thought. This is human nature, and I find it really beautiful when "family" happens in the Kingdom.

SPIRITUAL GRANDPARENTS

Recently Tim shared with us that the pastors have been looking for the grandparents in our body. I believe that the Lord is looking for the grandparents in His overall body. I would be amiss if I didn't address the very crucial subject of spiritual grandparents. What are spiritual grandparents, and what are some qualities needed that they offer? Just like in natural families, grandparents are essential to the total landscape of the family God desires. One of the gravest mistakes natural grandparents make is to try to play the role of parent instead of grandparent.

GRANDPARENT VS. PARENT

A grandparent does not have the same place as the parent. When a grandparent takes on the role of parent, a child is confused and often learns to play the parent against the grandparent. The child says, "But papaw (or whatever other term of endearment is used for grandpa) said I can do, eat, go" etc. Often marriages suffer when grandparents don't allow their children to parent their grandchildren. It doesn't matter if the parent is wrong in the eyes of their parent in dealing with the grandchild; the grandparent must not interfere. Now we realize that if there is a physical or other danger involved, that is a different matter. Parents have to allow their children to be parents, and too many times when the grandparent interferes, it results in chaos and can even facilitate breakups in marriages over issues that should never be addressed by grandparents. I've witnessed situations close to my heart where the in-laws become the outlaws if you would. Too sad! Think about this concept. You have two or even more sets of grandparents in a relationship. Who decides what is right in various situations? The right answer should be a resounding, "none of the grandparents!" So what should the role of the grandparent be? Pray for their children. Pray for their grandchildren. Spoil them. LOL! Do all the awesome things that grandparents do for their grandkiddos. Let the parents parent! So how does this apply in the area of spiritual parenting? Spiritual grandparents give and pour into their children and support them in fathering the children God has entrusted to them. This is huge! It is a very lacking thing in the body of Christ. People grow older, acquire wisdom, vast life experience, and then retire, move, and such. There is a reason that the Bible tells the older to teach the younger. One great reason is that the younger ones in our society have, in many places, tuned out the older generations. I say that this is much to their demise. We have so much to learn from our elders!

Birthday Club

When we were youth pastors, my wife and I had what we called a birthday club. We would take youth with us to a senior's home on their birthday and let wisdom flow from their lives. We had the senior tell us how they came to Christ, share some stories of how they grew up, were in the military, etc. I remember the youth kind of making fun of this idea when we first proposed it. But as it transpired, the youth told their friends that it is a very cool thing. There were a number of youth in a small home blessing a senior or senior couple and being blessed in return. So it is a crucial part of the kingdom family to embrace the elders in our lives. It is very crucial for the elders to understand the role they play and never underestimate how valuable they are in the Kingdom. There really isn't much if anything out there in the form of teaching, books, etc. about this role. Honestly, it's pretty undefined. That is why I addressed it here. Here are some big keys to remember in defining this in a spiritual sense. First and foremost, spiritual grandparents are necessary for the total fulfillment of God's heart for His family. Next, they need to understand that their life is not over, and they have fulfilled only part of their purpose. That doesn't mean they have to be as active as when they were younger. However, it does mean they play some role in being spiritual mentors. Another key is to know that their role is to support their spiritual children as they grow and mentor the children in their lives. It is not, however, the place of the spiritual grandparent to father the grandchild. There has to be room for error and even some pretty major mistakes to be made by the spiritual parent. That is how we learned and exactly the same way that they will. God will protect our spiritual children and grandchildren from our mistakes. Larry Randolph, a friend I've mentioned earlier in this book, understands this well. He said that when God created the plans for our lives, he factored in all the wrong turns and bad decisions we would make along the way. This whole thing is an awesome cycle, and one that is near to God's heart.

Fathering and Being Fathered

Fathering is not meant to be a stop-go relationship. At its finest, fathering includes both being fathered and, ultimately, always fathering. We have a wealth poured into us, and then we pour into others and teach them to do the same. As we learned from what I call the "Judges 2:10 Generation," when fathering (even at its most incredible display) fails to continue forward, generations can be lost. Therefore, an ultimate standard of an ultimate son or daughter is that they become an even greater spiritual father or mother!

On the surface, it would be so easy to ask, "How could such powerful and long-term training produce anything less than another great father?" But we continue to see in Christian history that great training doesn't guarantee another great father. We have to be intentional about a vision to carry on greatness to future generations. Therefore, I challenge you to become not only an ultimate spiritual son or daughter, but also a great father or mother.

THE QUALITIES OF THE "ULTIMATES"

What are some hallmarks of ultimate fathers and ultimate sons? These are a few earmarks of each:

ULTIMATE SONS
- Seek to hear God for everything in your life
- Work through times when you feel you are hearing one thing from God while your leader is hearing something else
- Remain teachable
- Resist the urge to validate and defend yourself to your leaders
- Are open to the fact that you don't see everything clearly (expect blind-spots to be revealed and addressed)
- Know that your fathers aren't perfect
- Pray for your father's family
- Don't use the "I have more wisdom than my teachers, have the Holy Spirit to guide me, etc." excuses to live outside of a mentoring relationship
- Trust the Lord in the process
- Trust the leaders the Lord has placed over your life
- Value your mentor's time
- Follow leaders as they follow Christ
- Honor leaders in any way you are able, including blessing them financially
- Sacrifice to be a part of *their* schedule
- Understand that if you ask a leader to speak into your life but then ignore their counsel, you will most likely lose their input in the future
- Don't bring multiple fathers into your life to create multiple voices so you can find one that always agrees with you
- Live a life of submission to authority
- Never criticize your fathers to others
- Cover your father's weaknesses
- Carry your father's anointings

- Find people to father you that you know "truly" have your best interest and God's heart for you in mind
- Learn to love their correction
- If you've been wounded by leaders, don't give up on all of them. They are still central to God's heart for seeing your destiny fulfilled.
- Become unoffendable
- Recognize that the heart of God is first toward a person, and then their ministry. Invite leaders into your life who value you before they value your gifting. These are the types of leaders who will help guide your destiny.
- Read/study books, messages, etc. as recommended by your fathers
- Don't give up on the process
- Trust that your leaders can see pages or chapters ahead in your life because God gives them insight into it
- This relationship takes time and doesn't just happen
- Are a learner and not a teacher when with your fathers
- Are intentional with being fathered
- Believe that you will never become who you are fully meant to be until you invite and embrace fathers in your life
- Learn the heart of your fathers
- Learn the passion and call of your fathers and how you can serve them
- Joyfully obey those over you
- Pray for those over you
- Don't let anyone speak ill of your fathers
- Always be growing
- Always be in both fathered and fathering roles

Ultimate Fathers
- Hear God for everything in your life and your sons
- Lead through love
- Don't use your authority to control, but rather to empower
- Always be growing as a father

- Continue to cultivate relationships
- Believe in your sons
- Pray for your sons
- Model and train them in the works of the Kingdom
- Find scriptures and identify prophetic truths about your sons, and pray them over them regularly
- Challenge your sons
- Recognize your sons' gifts and help them grow
- Get God's heart for your sons
- Equip them
- Release them
- Honor them
- Encourage them
- Bring loving correction
- Don't be codependent with them
- Allow them to make mistakes
- Give them assignments and trust them
- Don't step in and rescue them if you think they may be failing
- Trust the process of God in their lives
- Take them with you and allow them to watch you live life
- Be real
- Be transparent
- Teach them to be fathers
- Teach them to understand and practice the cycle of fathering and being fathered

I want to thank you personally for your attention and your heart as you have searched these pages for wisdom. In closing, I must share something that I feel like the Holy Spirit spoke to me as I was concluding this work. I was pondering the mystery and the privilege of becoming a father to a precious person in His Kingdom. I felt that He said to me, "I am the one who places sons and fathers. I bring them into your life, and I am the One who helps you father them." We are on a journey. The journey is one that involves becoming an ultimate son or daughter and also becoming an ultimate spiritual parent. Moving forward, pray about who should be fathering you, and also whom you should be fathering. Finding fathers and sons is the ultimate!

About the Author

Patrick Davis has been married to his beloved wife Marcia for 40 years. They have an amazing son and daughter who are both married to great spouses. All six of them attend the same church together, Grace Fellowship in Cabot, Arkansas. Pat and his family have been actively involved in the church for over 22 years. He has been a part of many ministries and has led several. Pat has been teaching and preaching for over 40 years. His heart is to see the body of Christ mature and become all that Jesus desires.